AUTUMN BEAUTY
Grayscale Photo Coloring Book

Anne Manera

Book design & Cover art
By Anne Manera

Photographs sourced from Pixabay

ISBN: 1537494031
ISBN-13: 978-1537494036

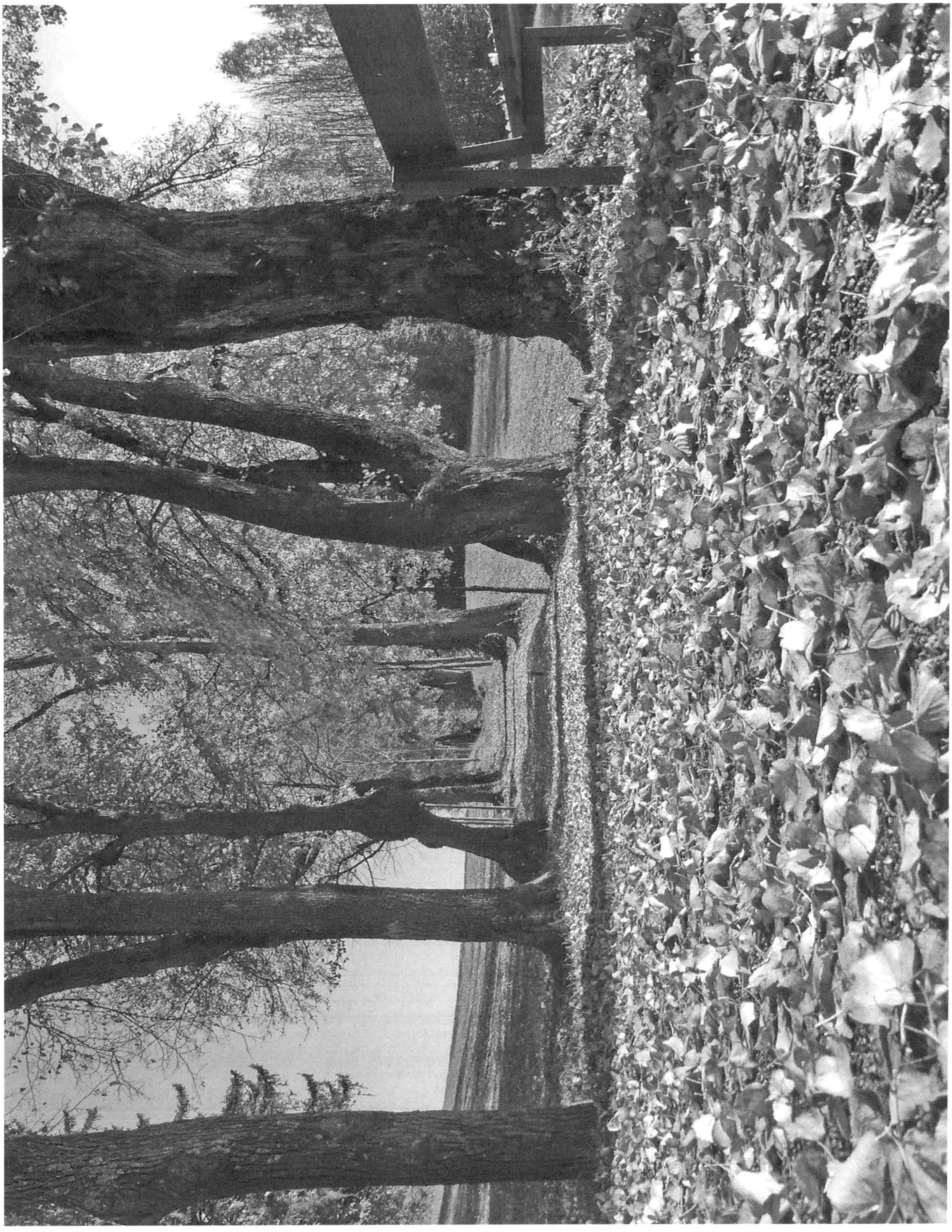

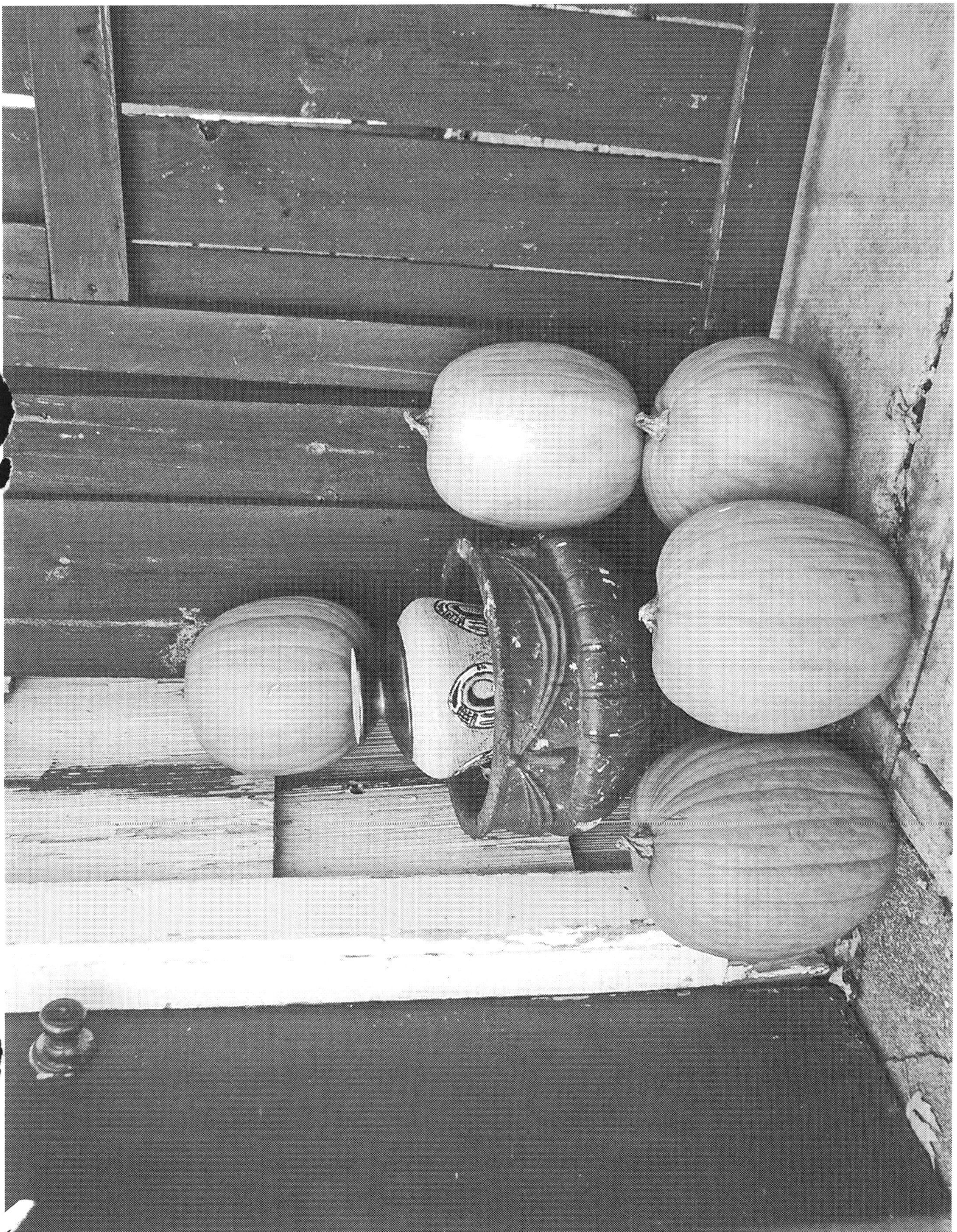

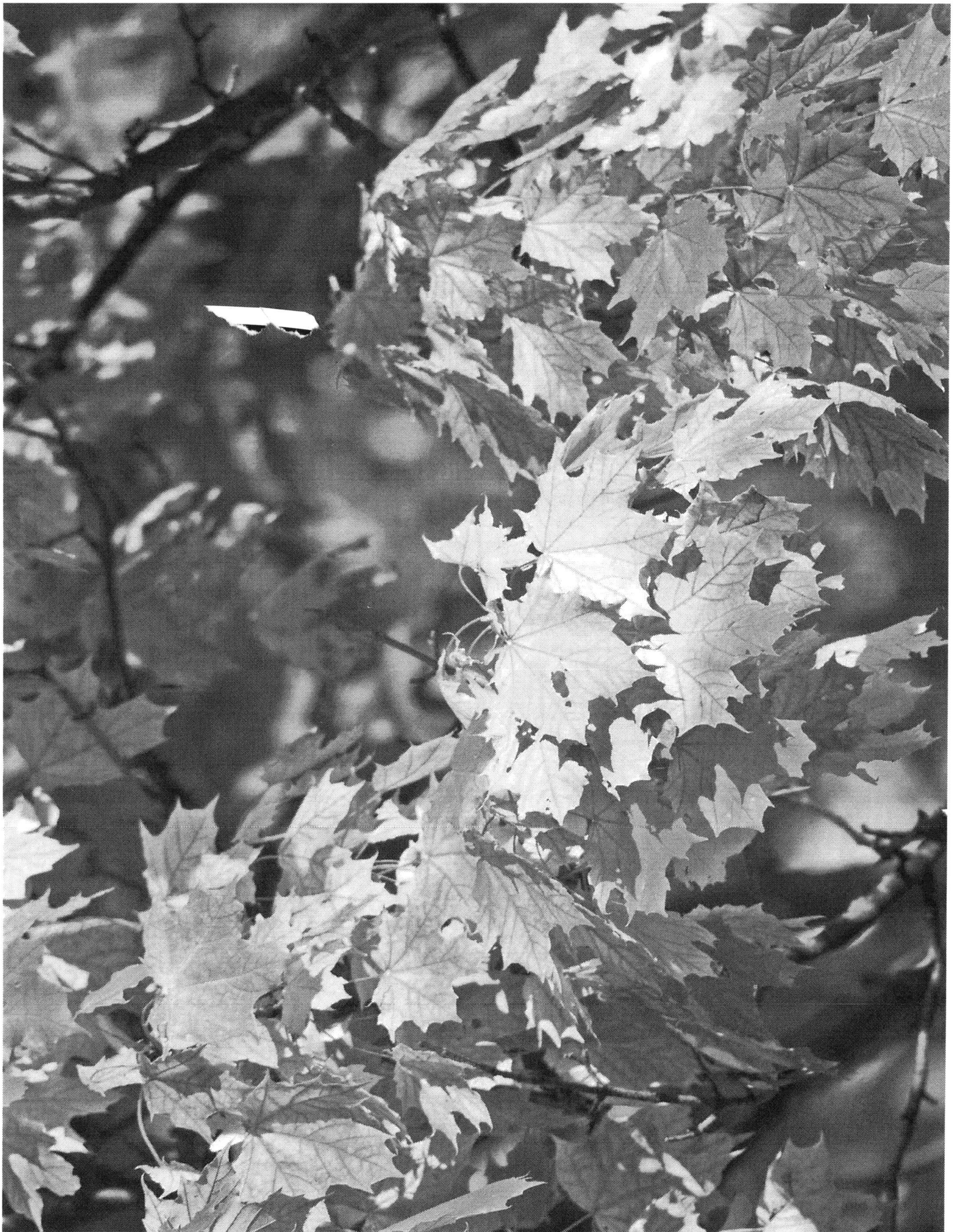

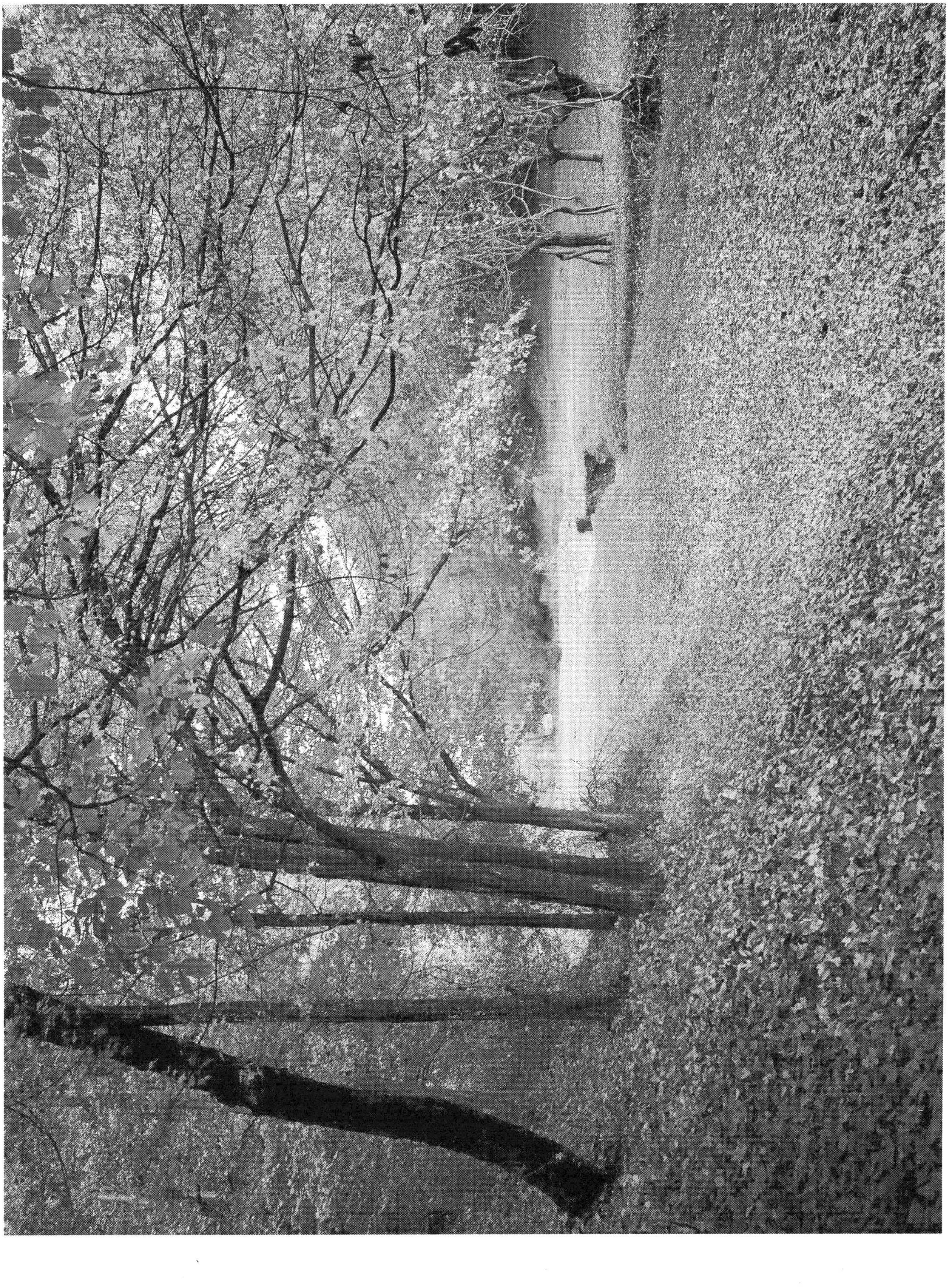

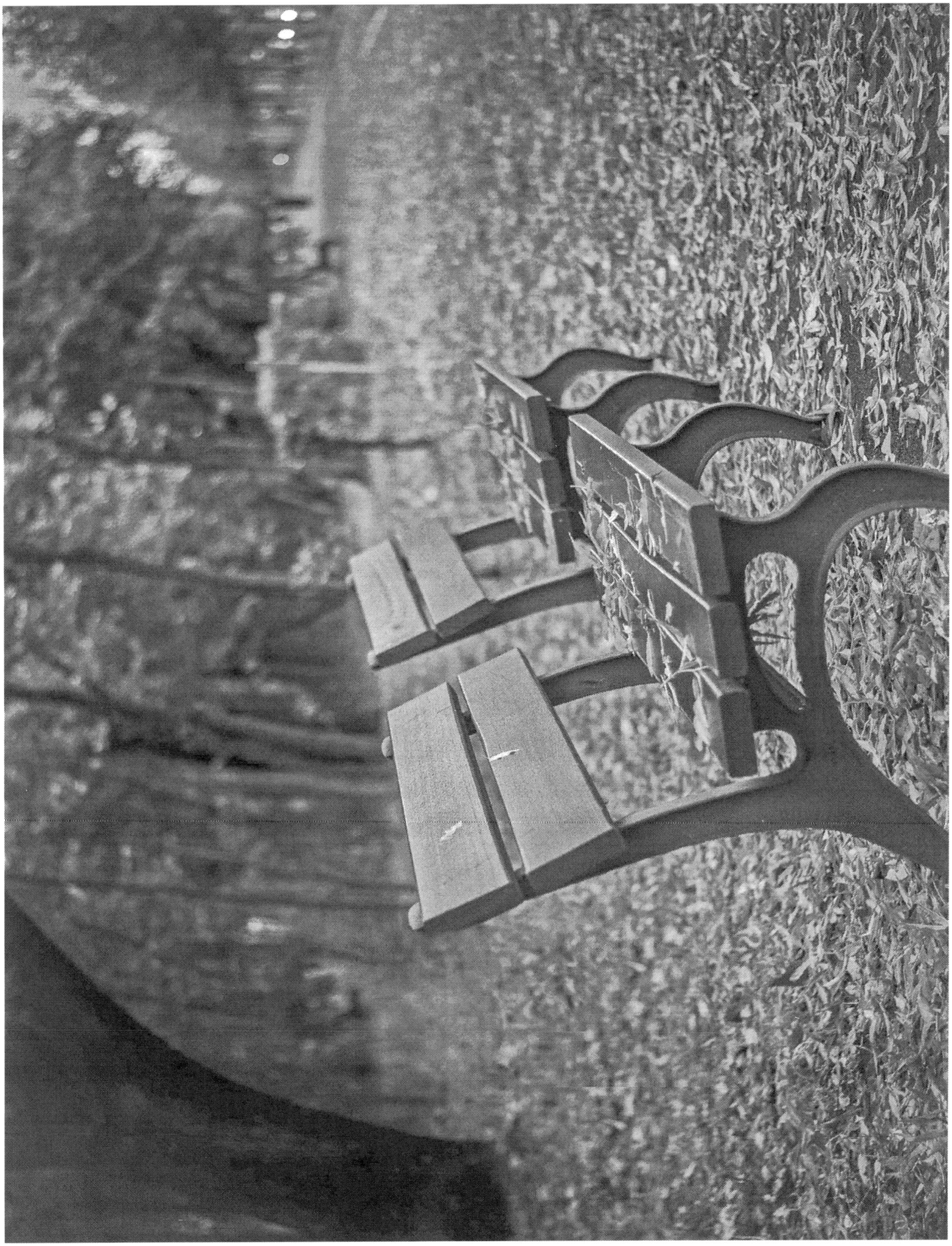

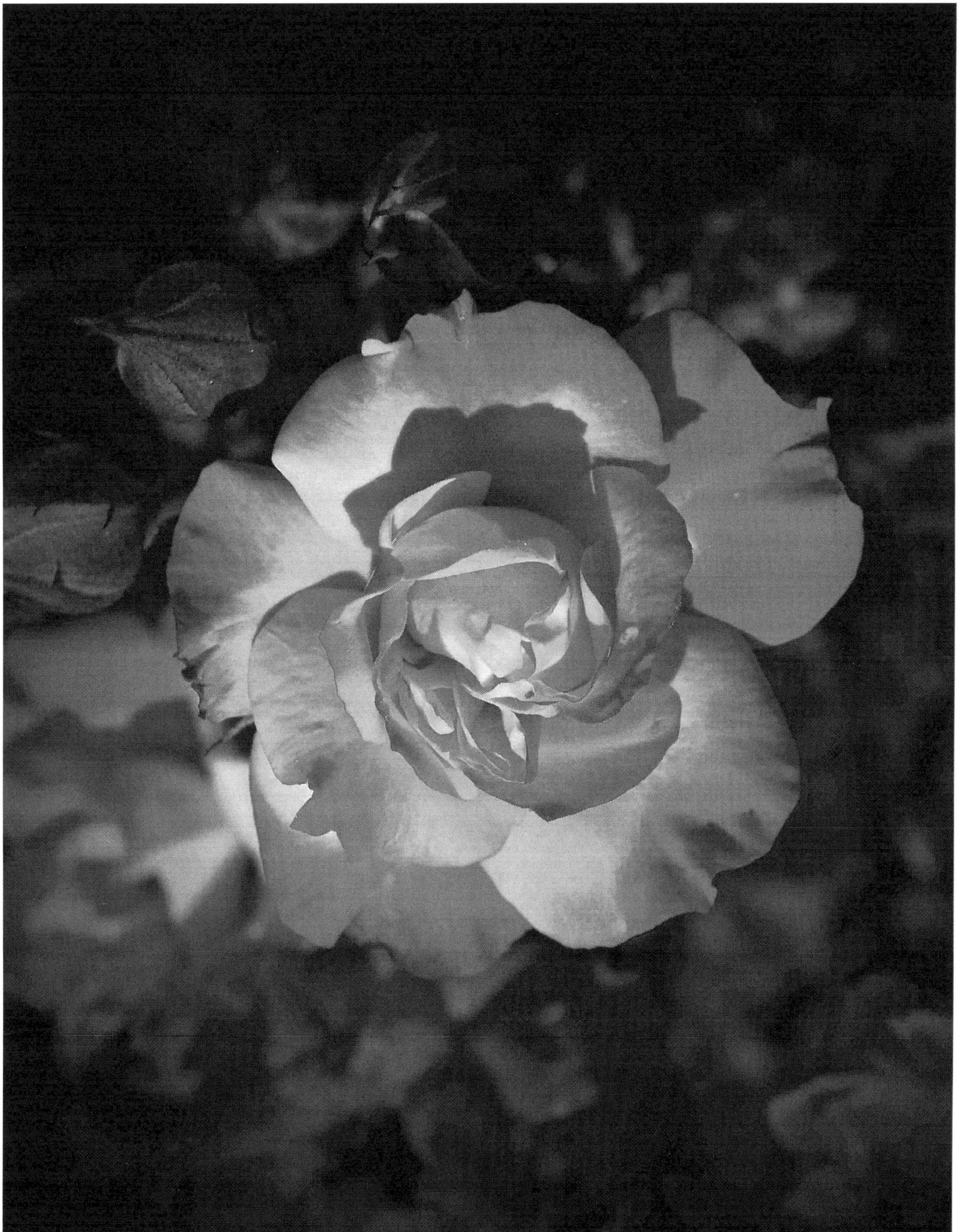

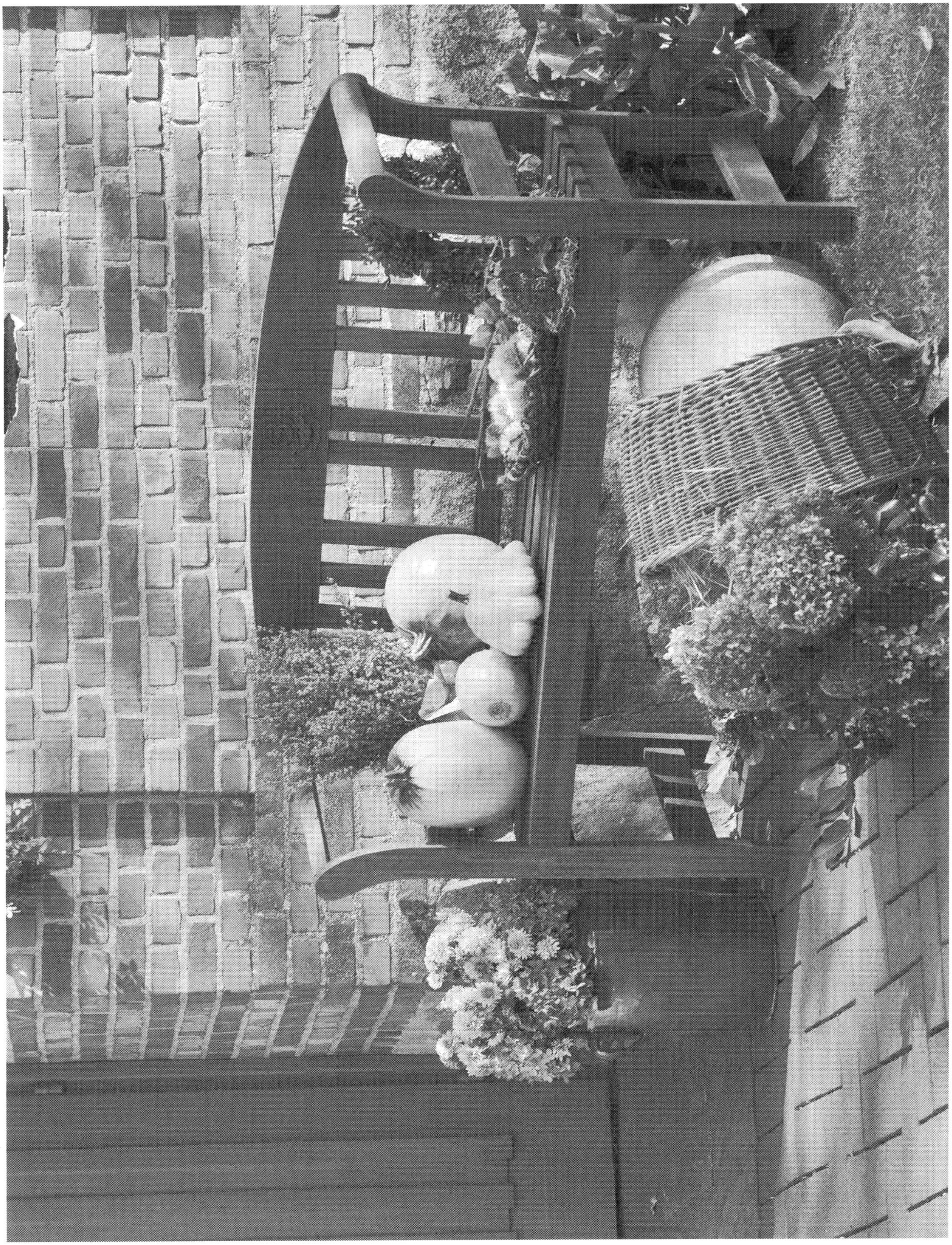

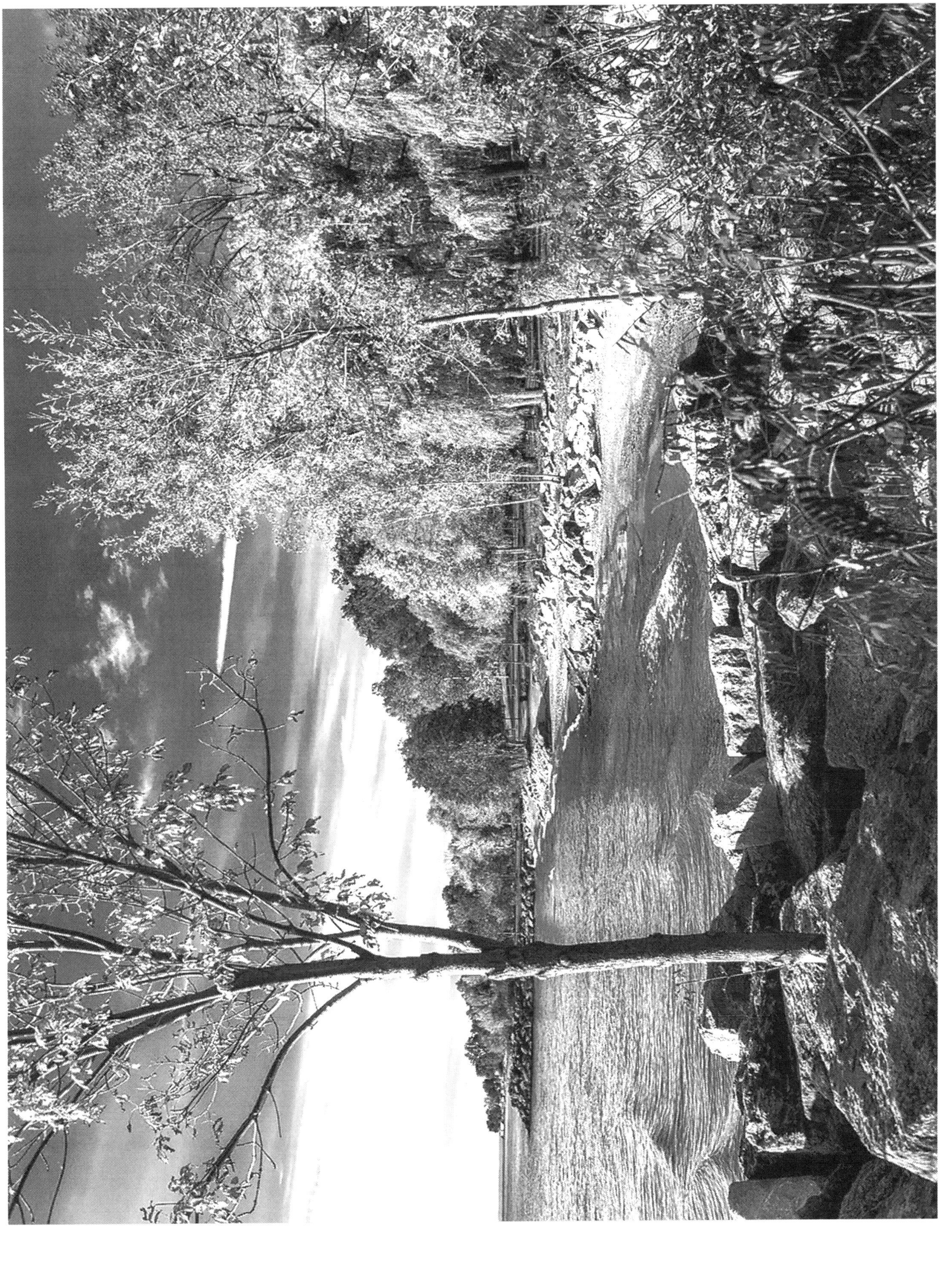

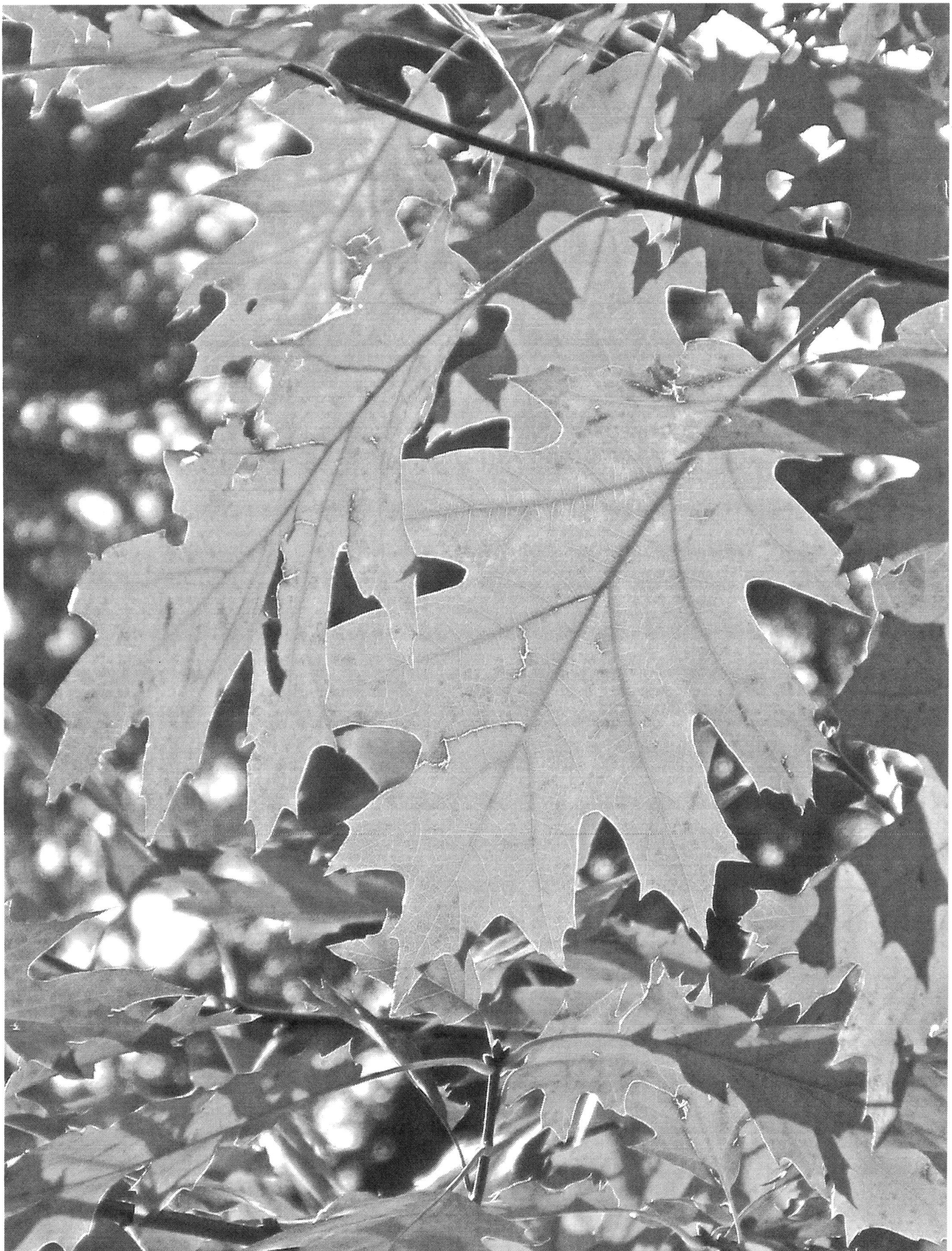

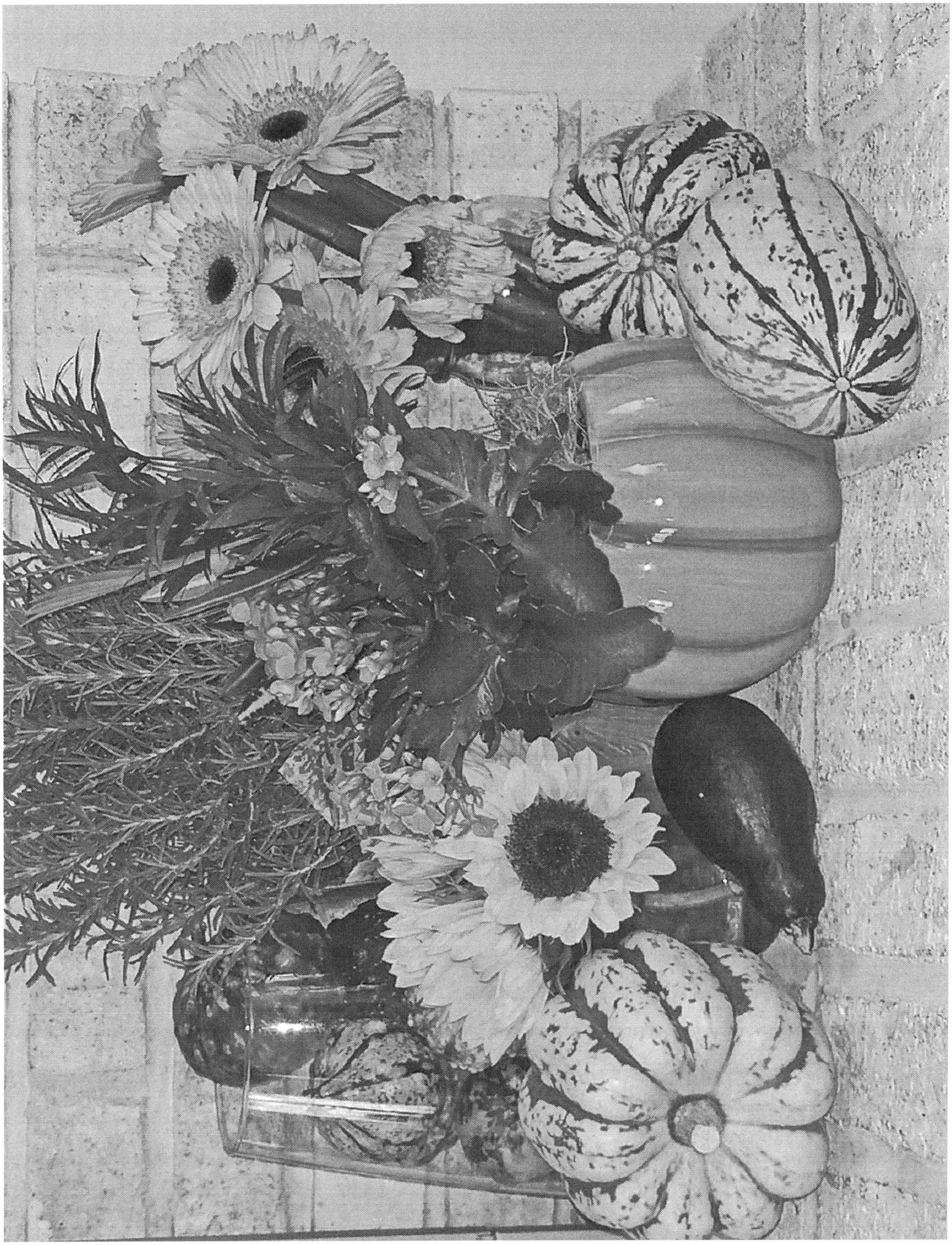

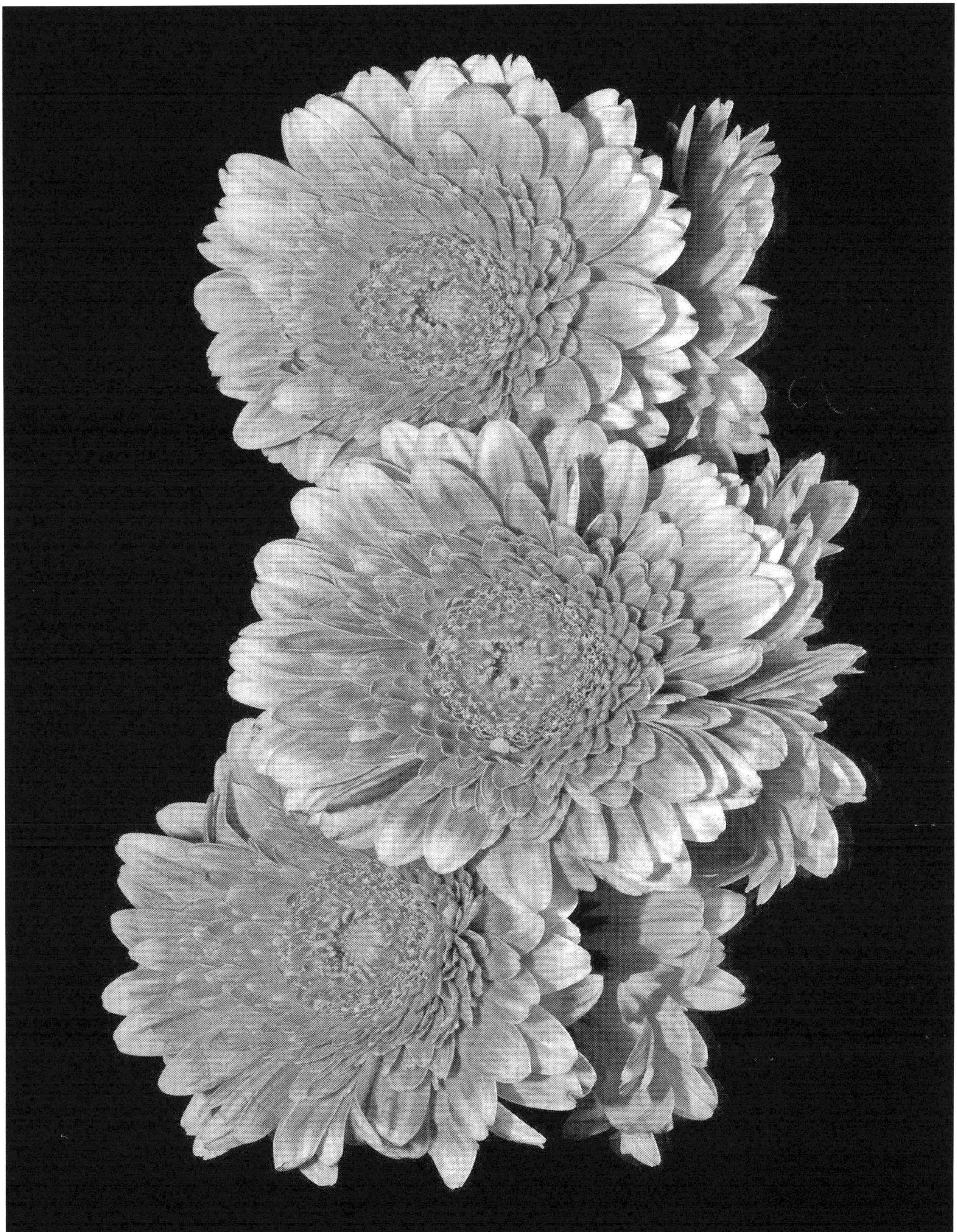

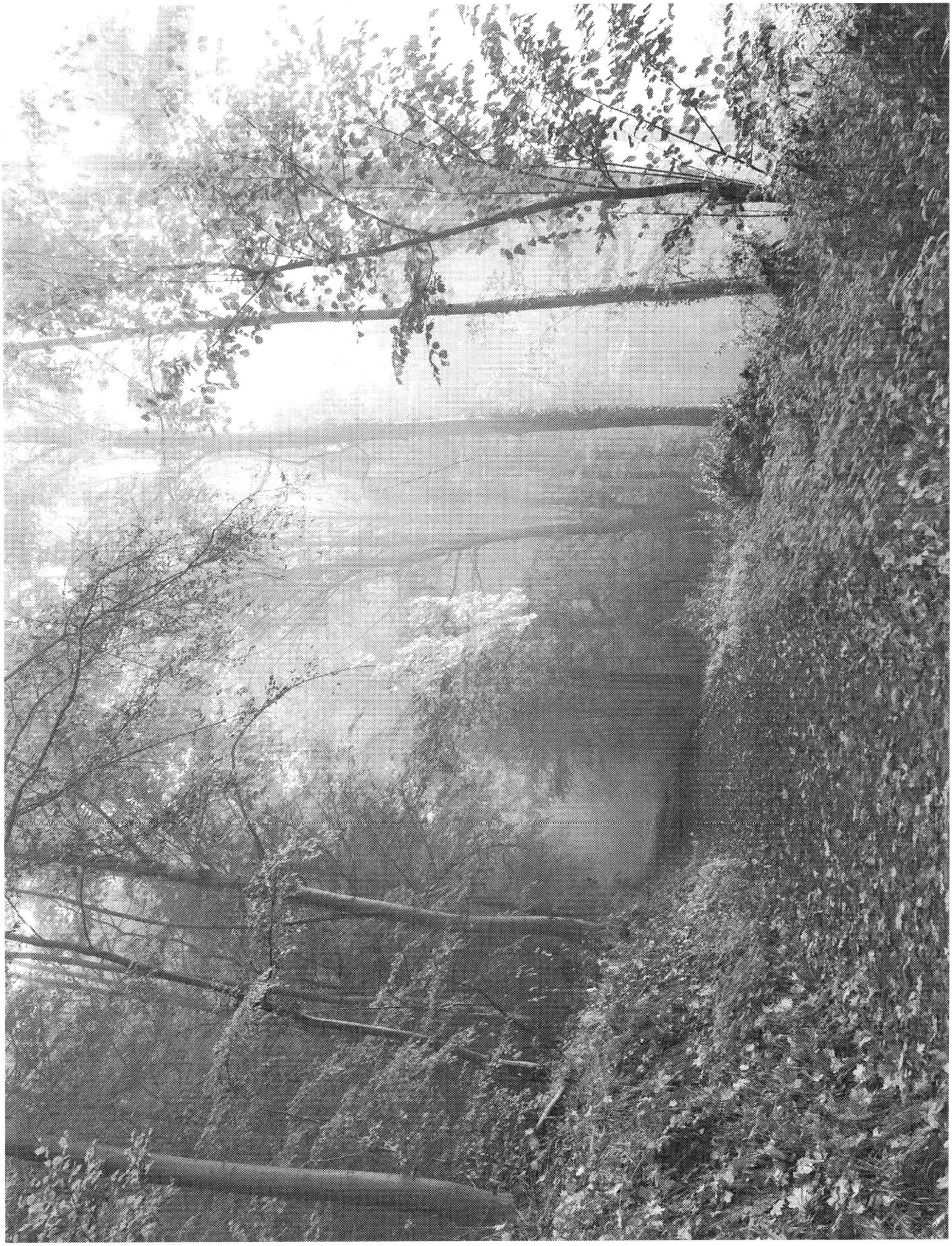

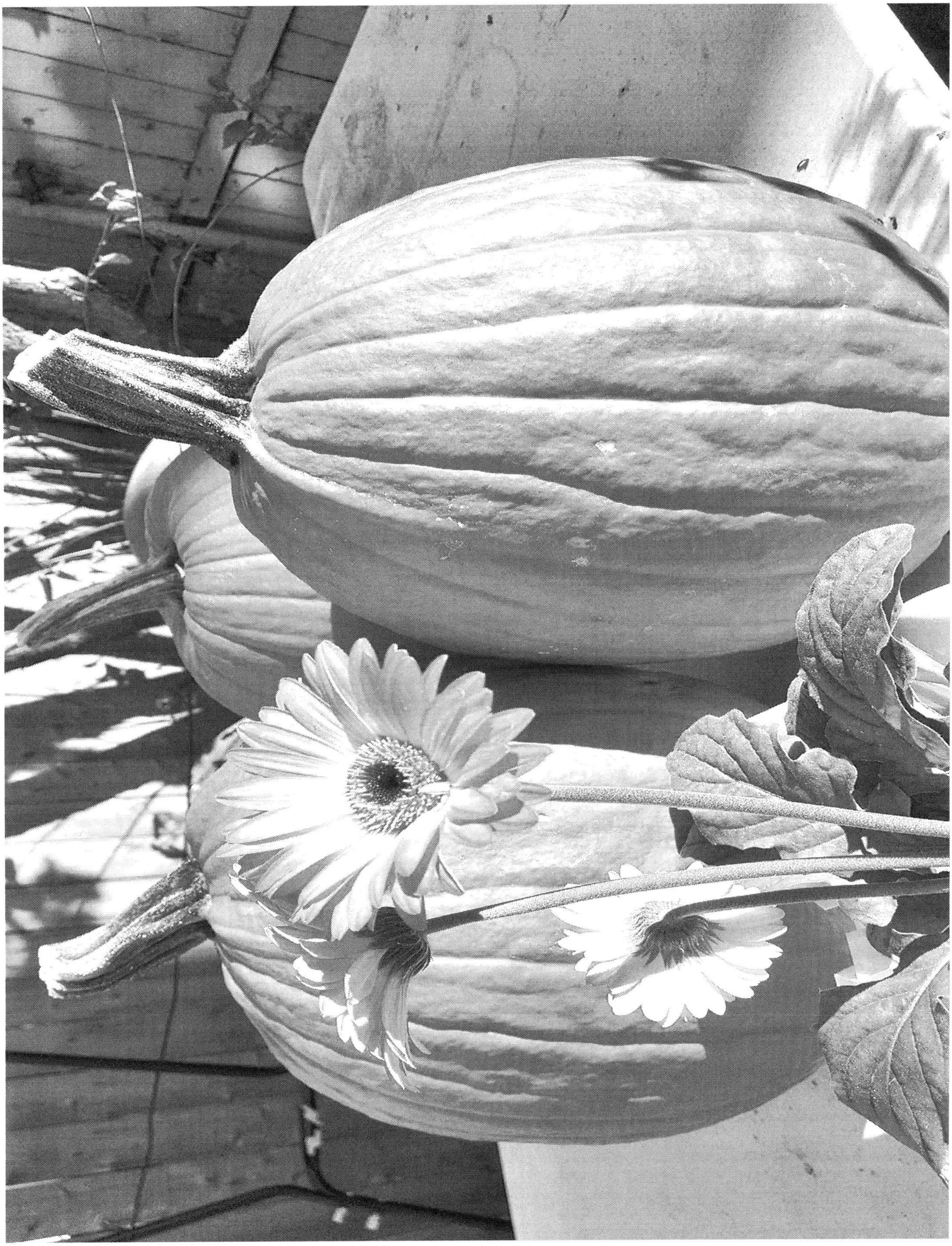

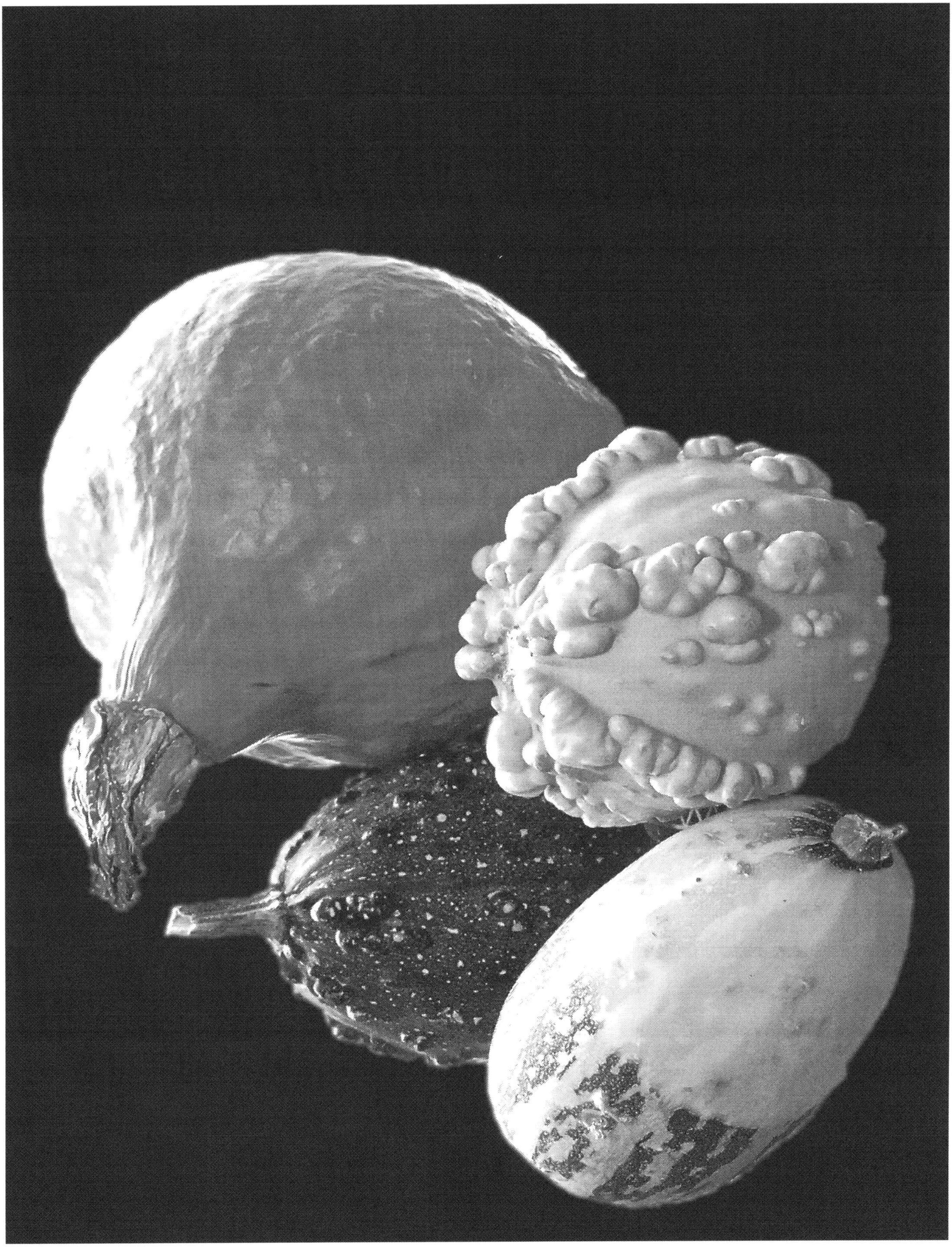

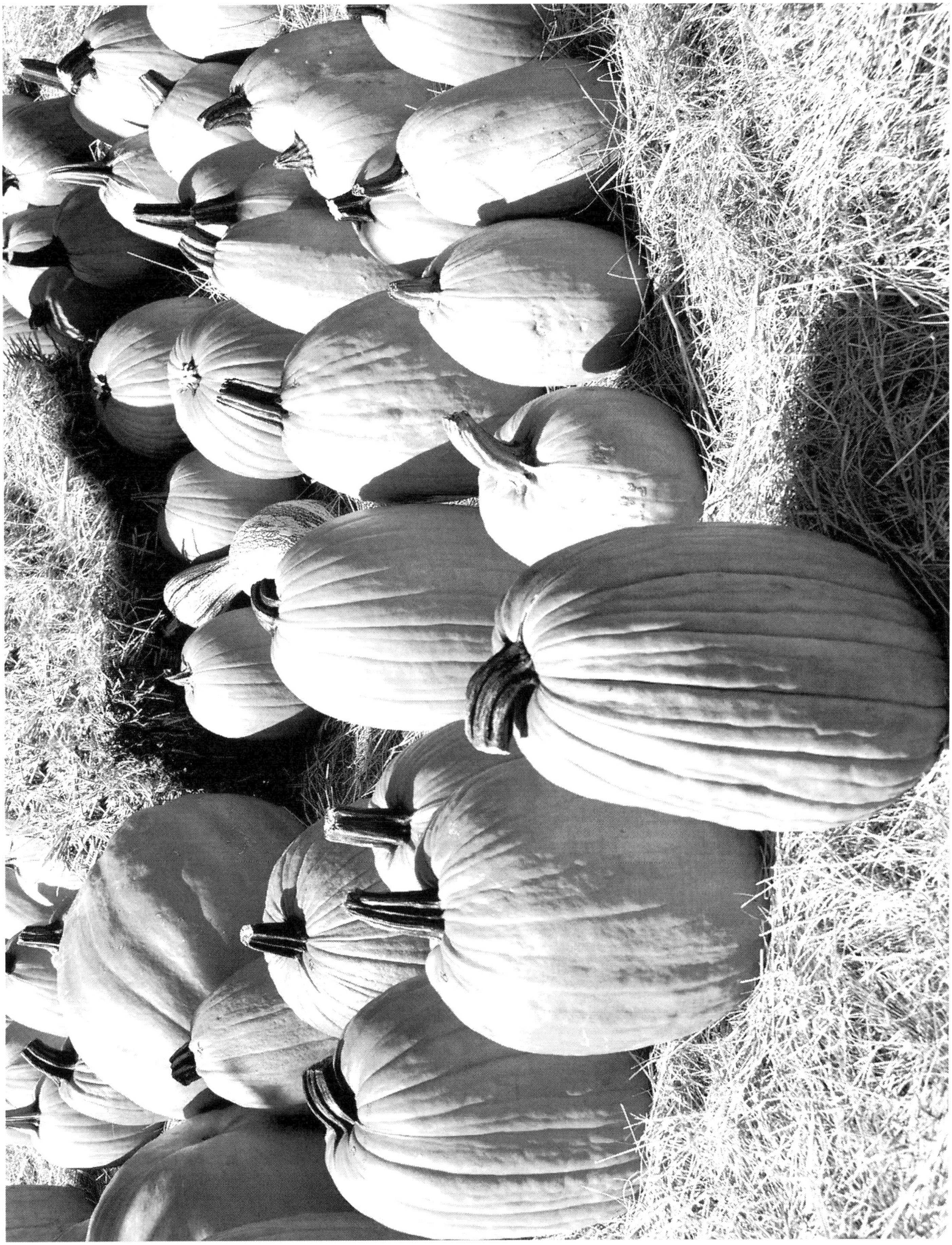

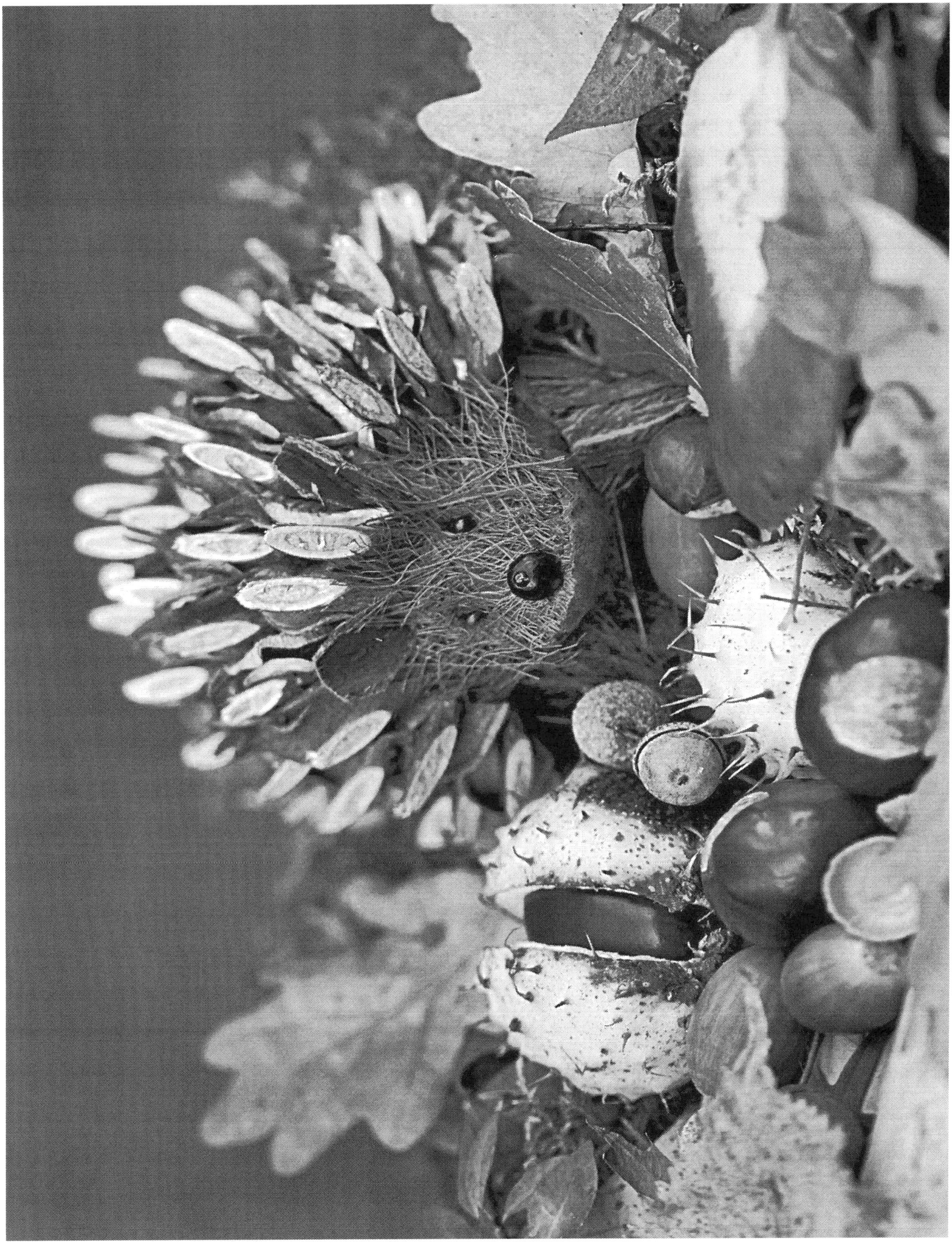

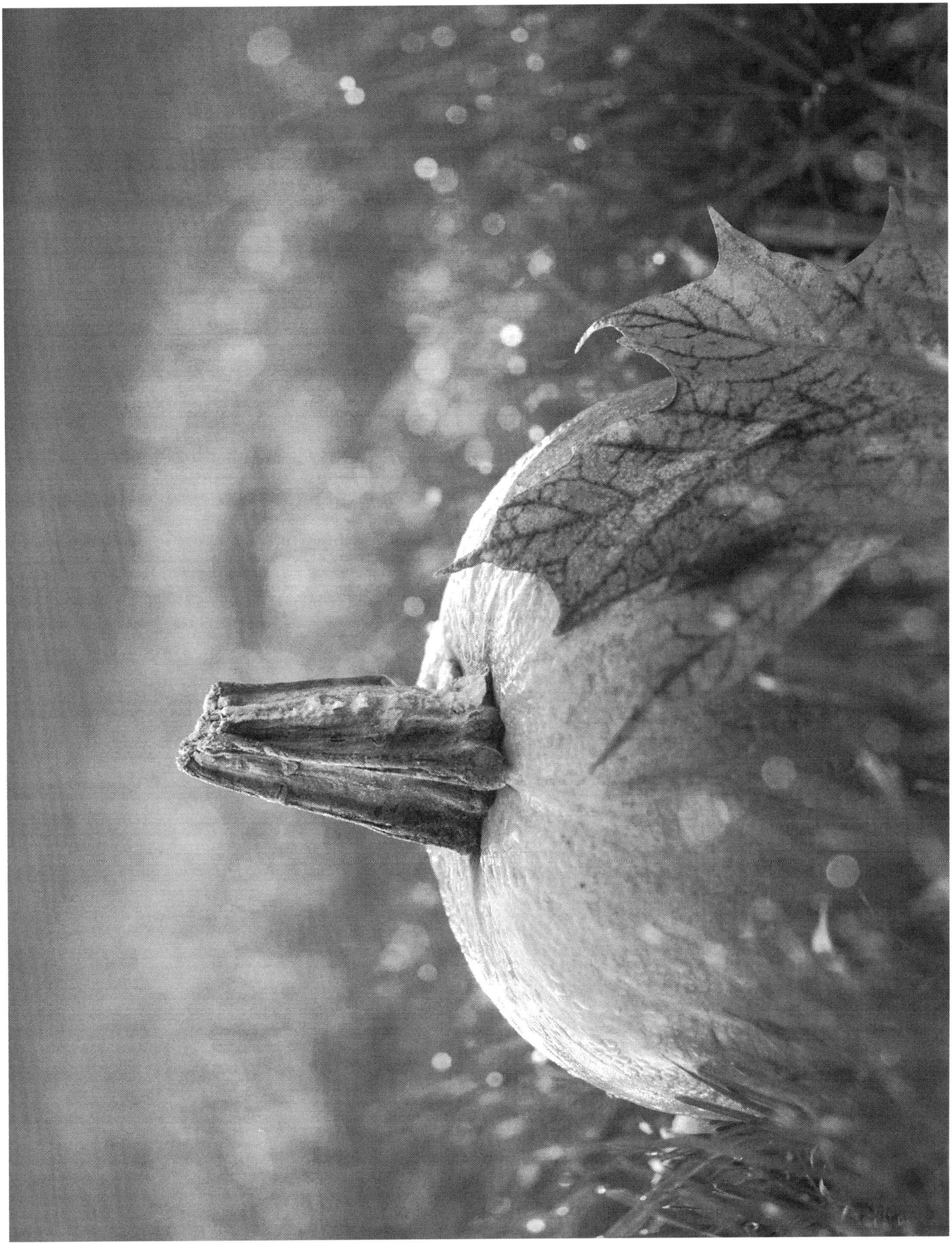

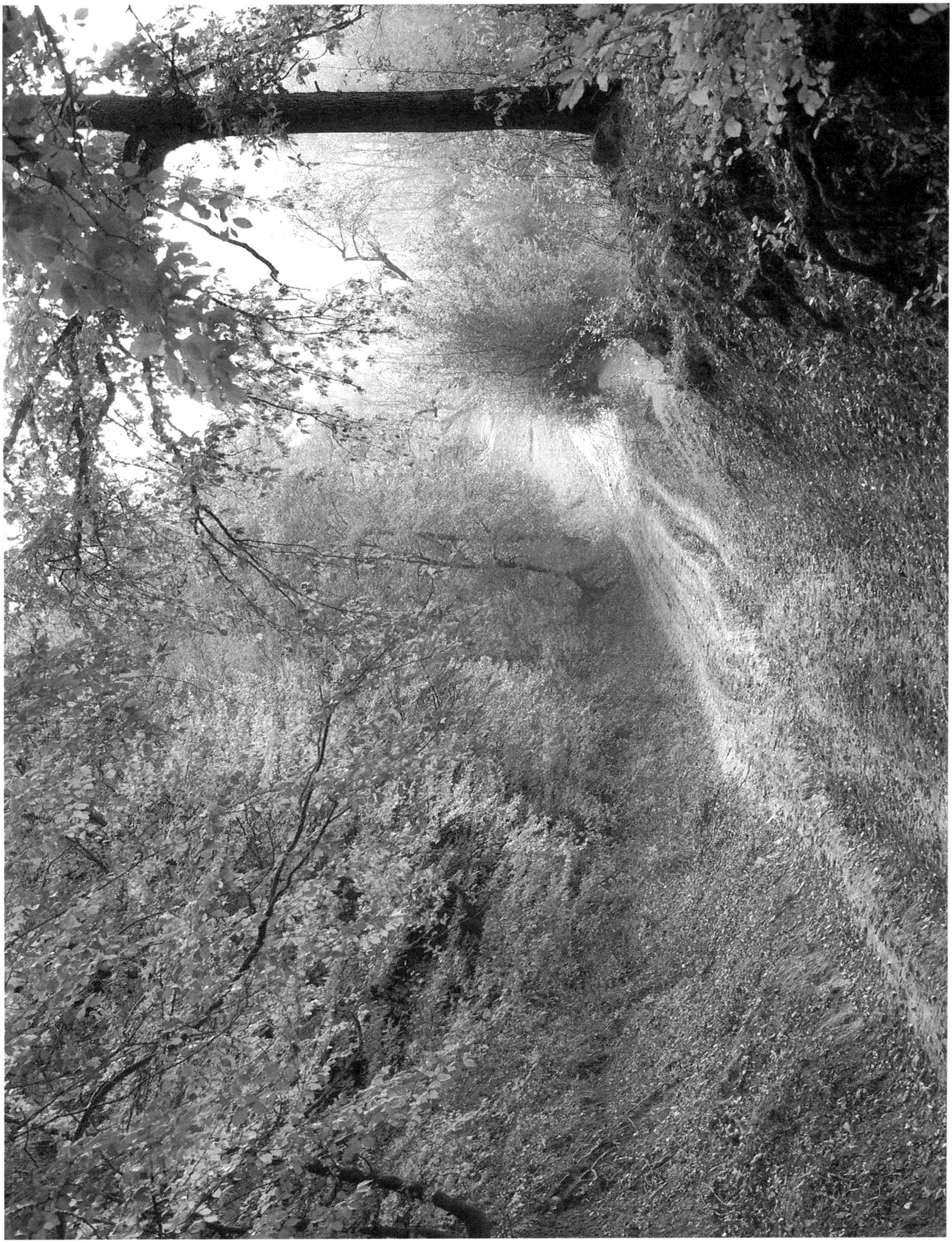

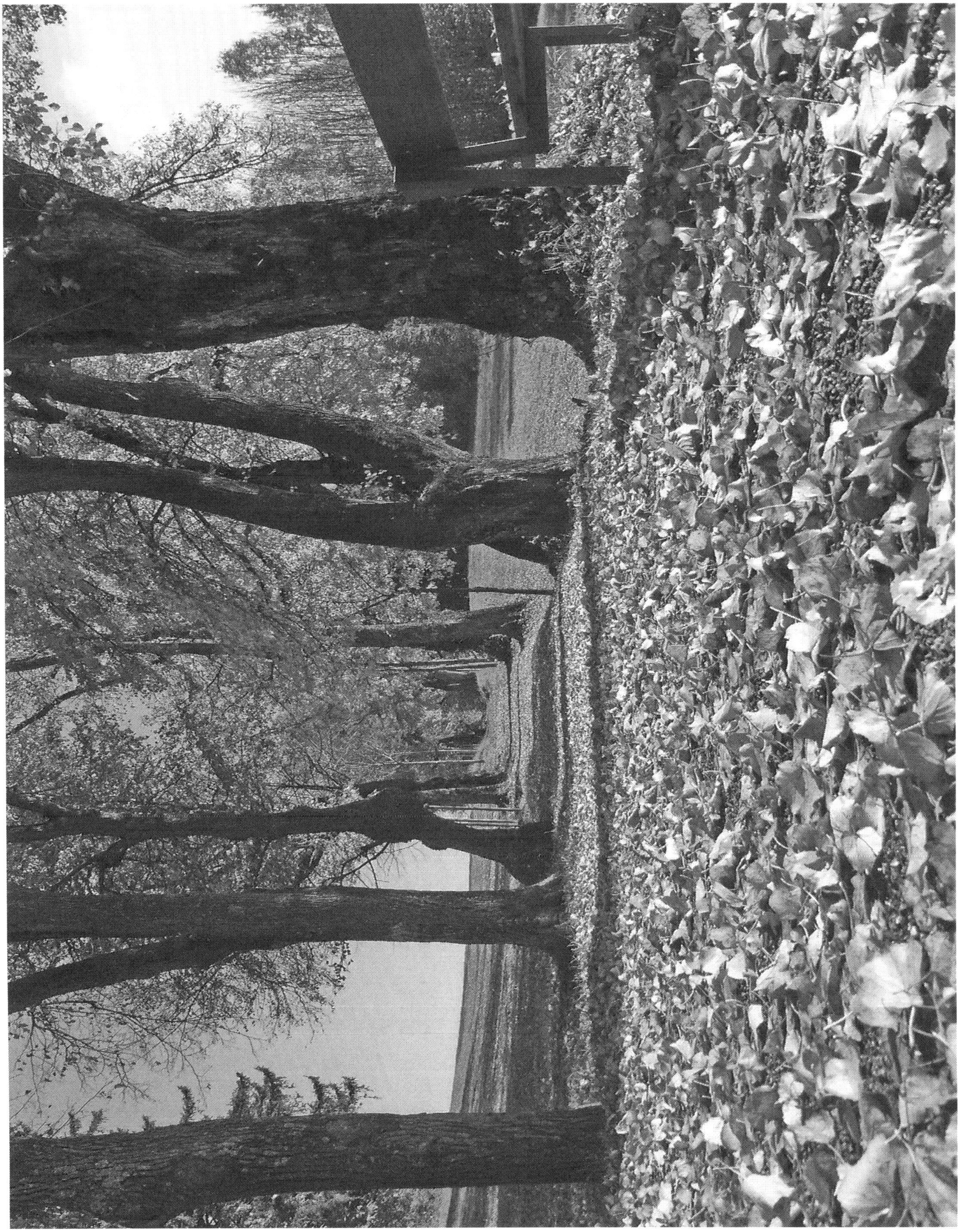

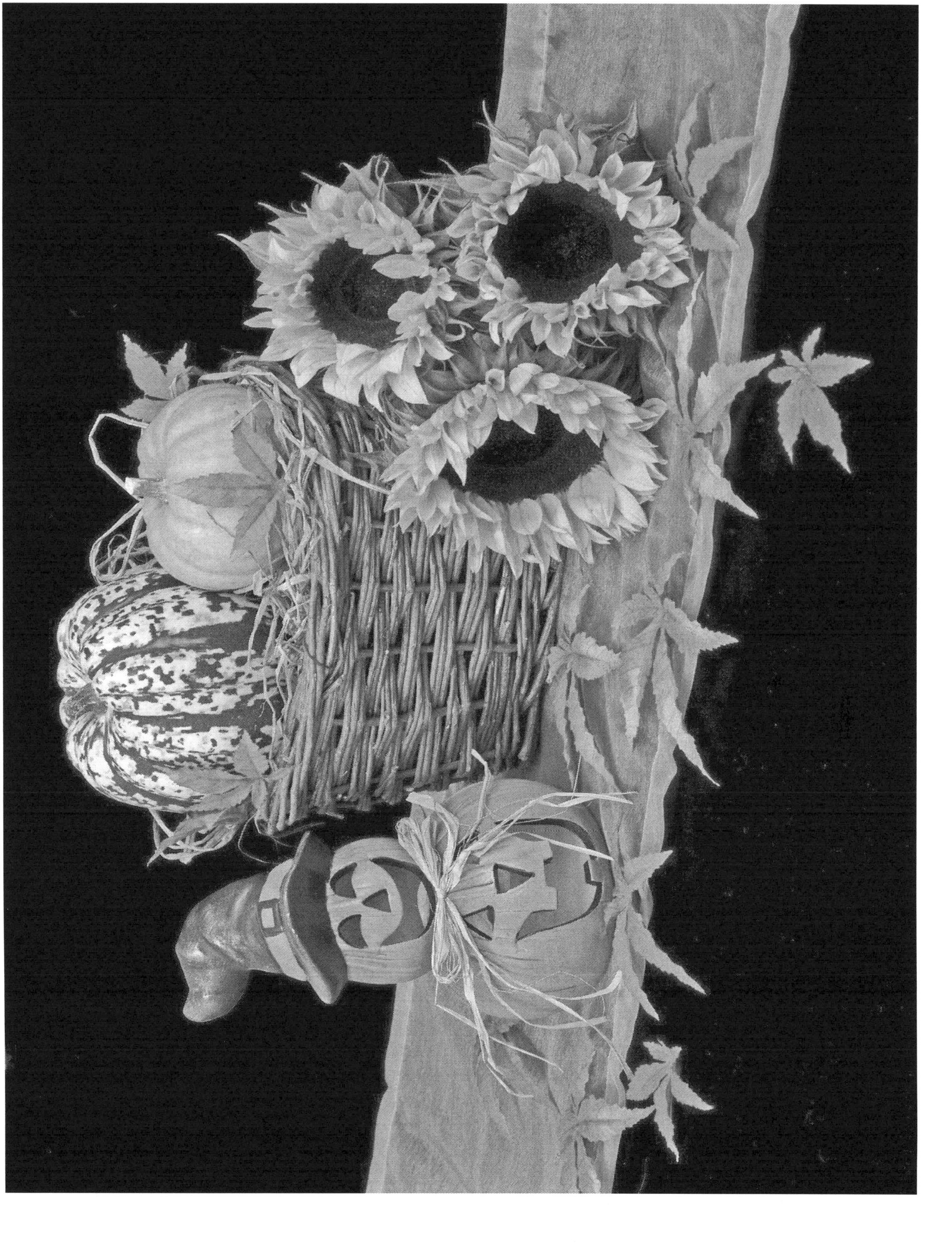

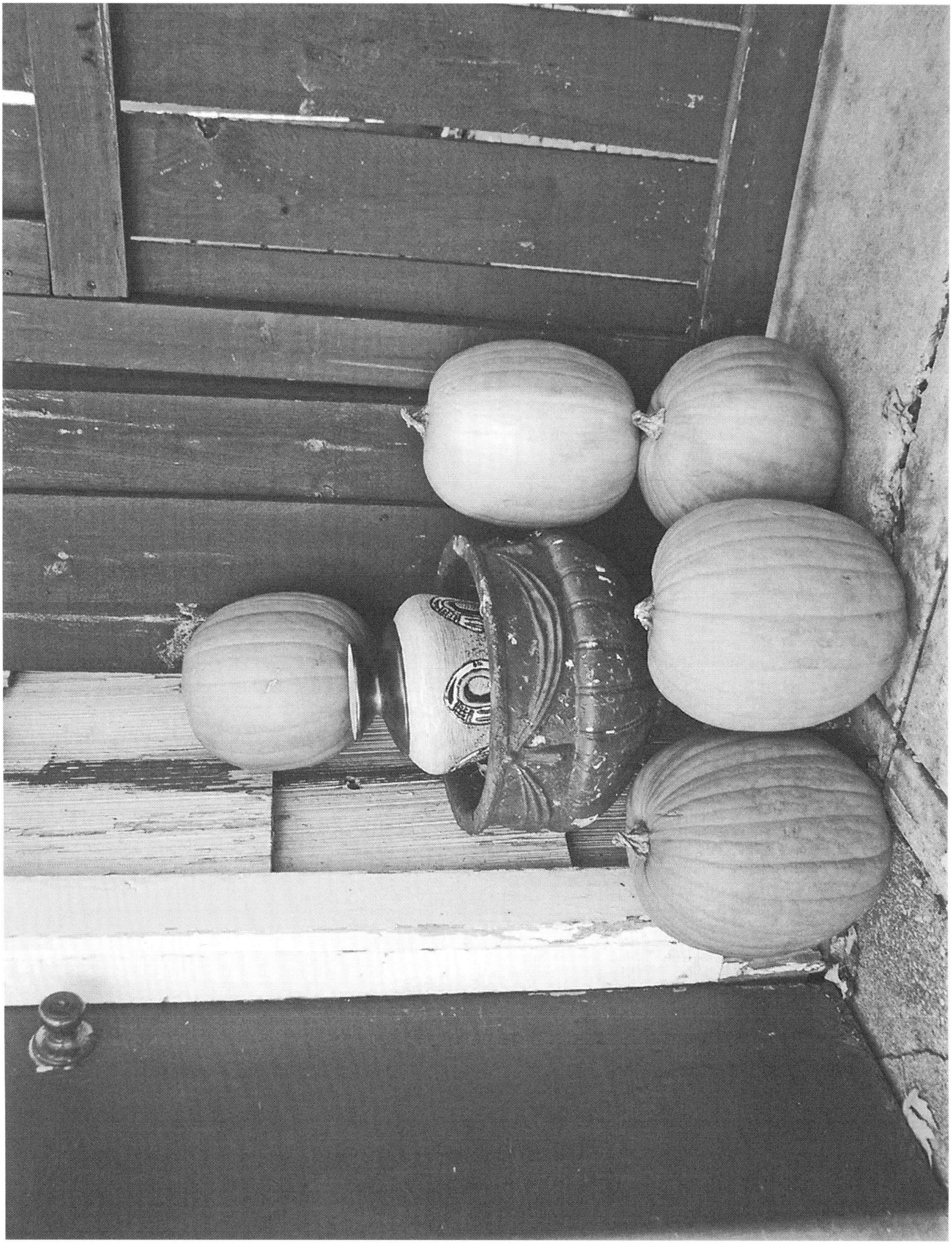

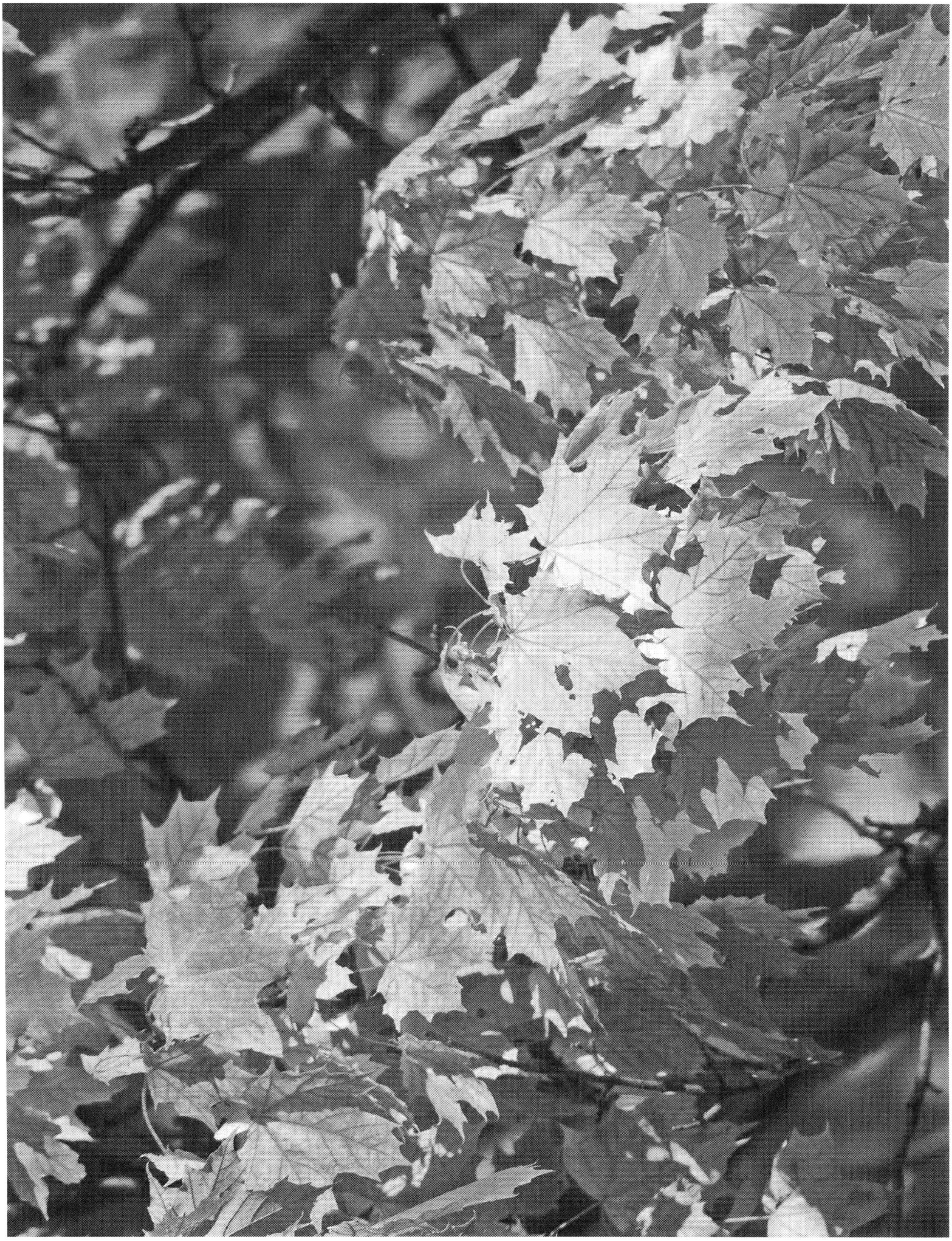

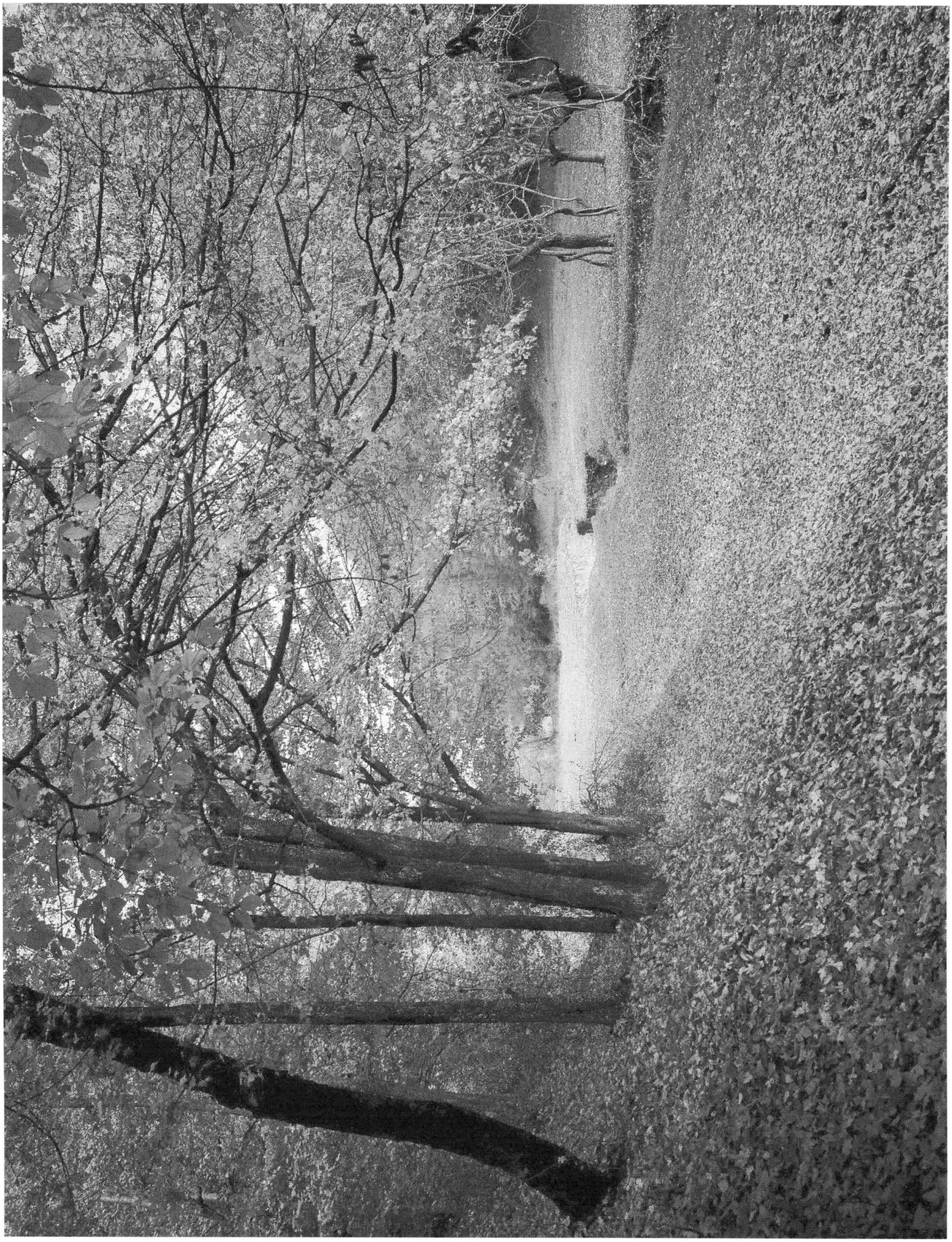

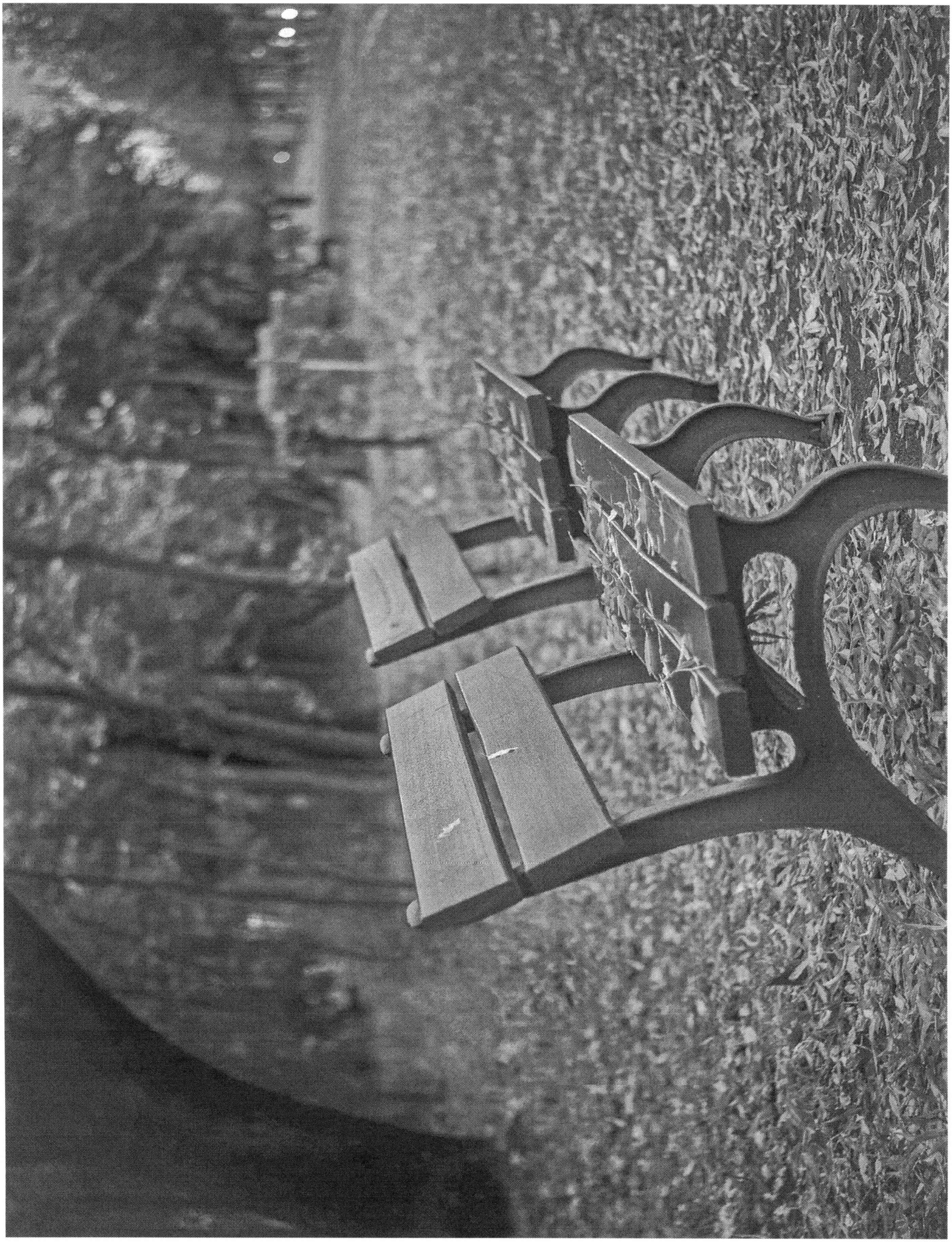

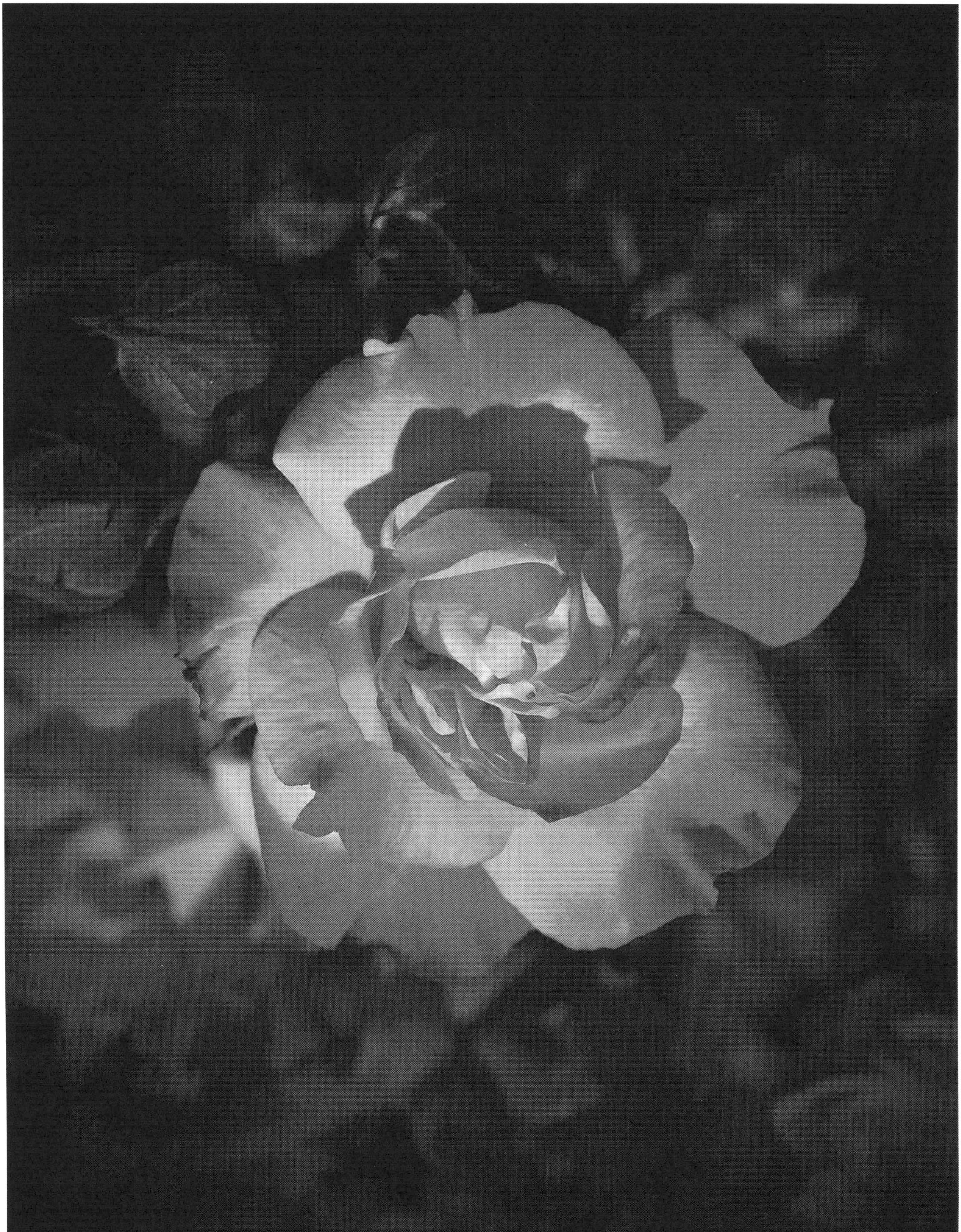

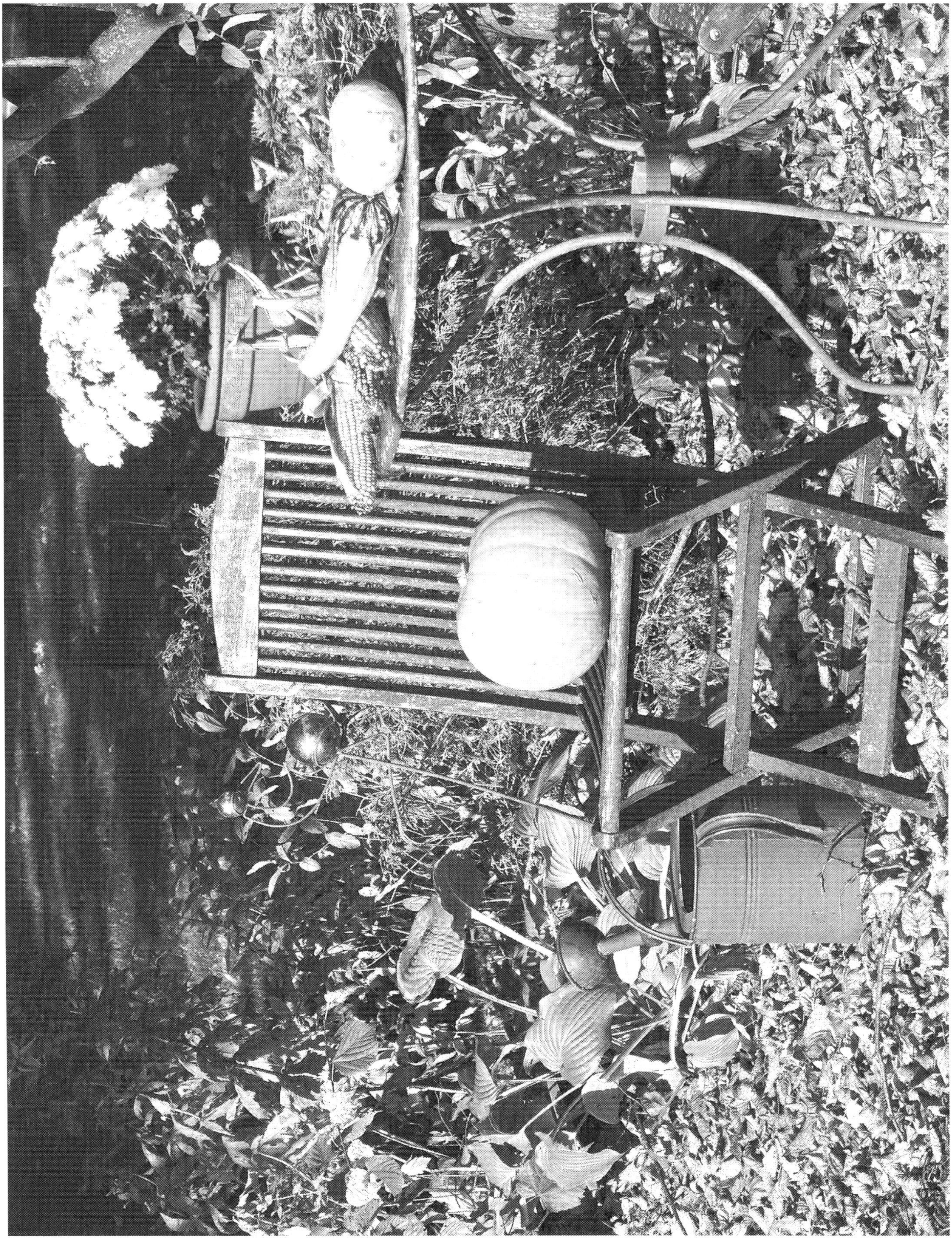

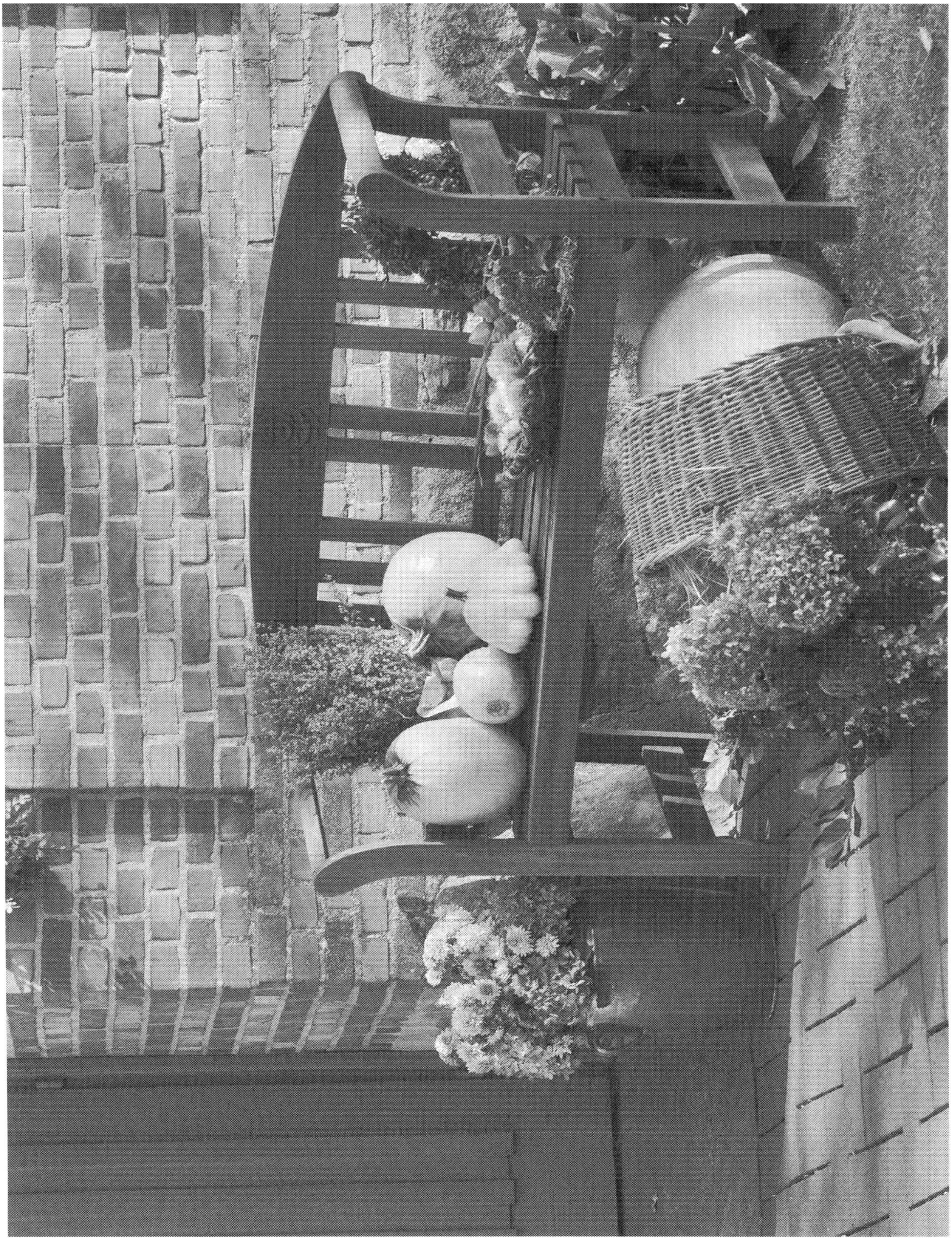

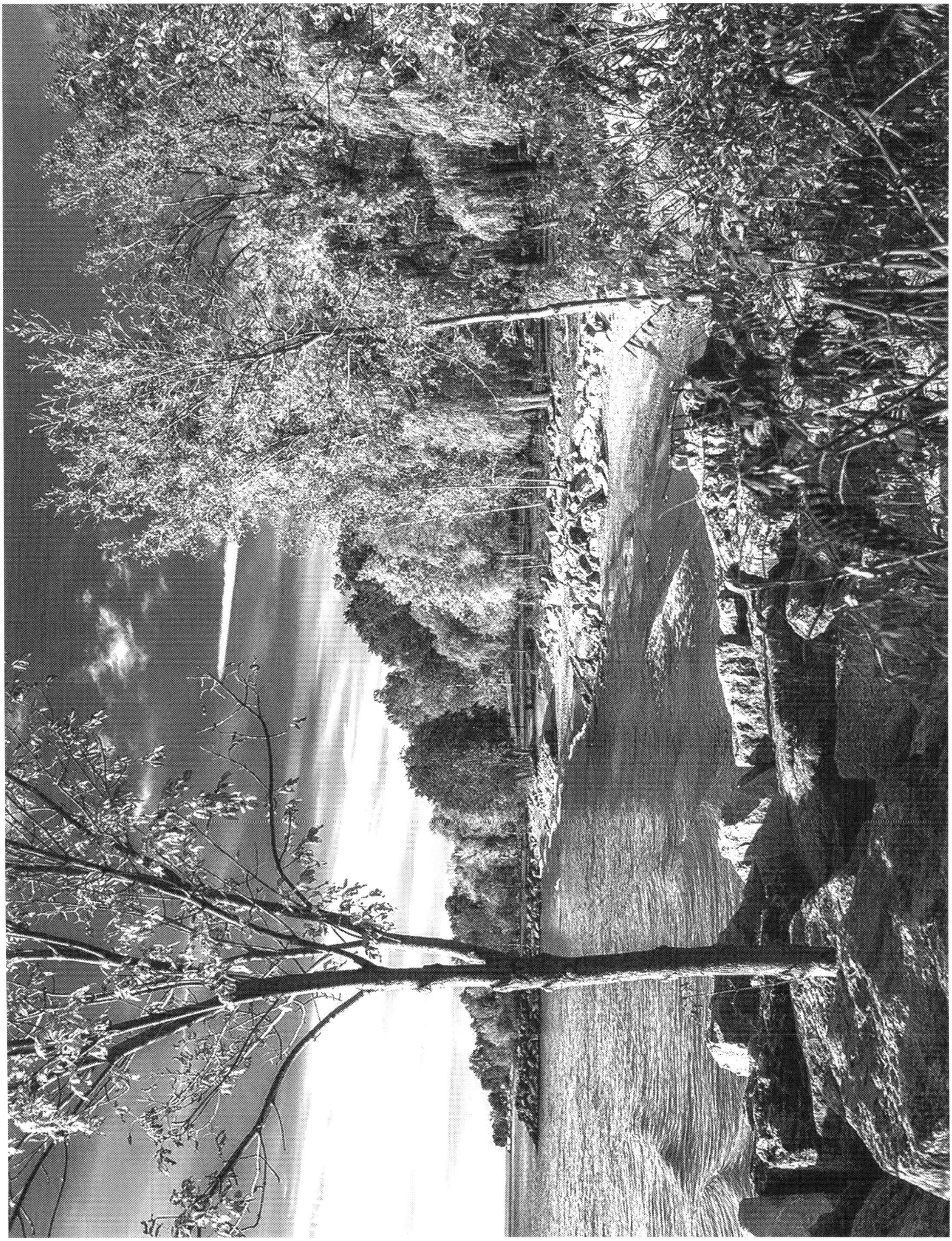

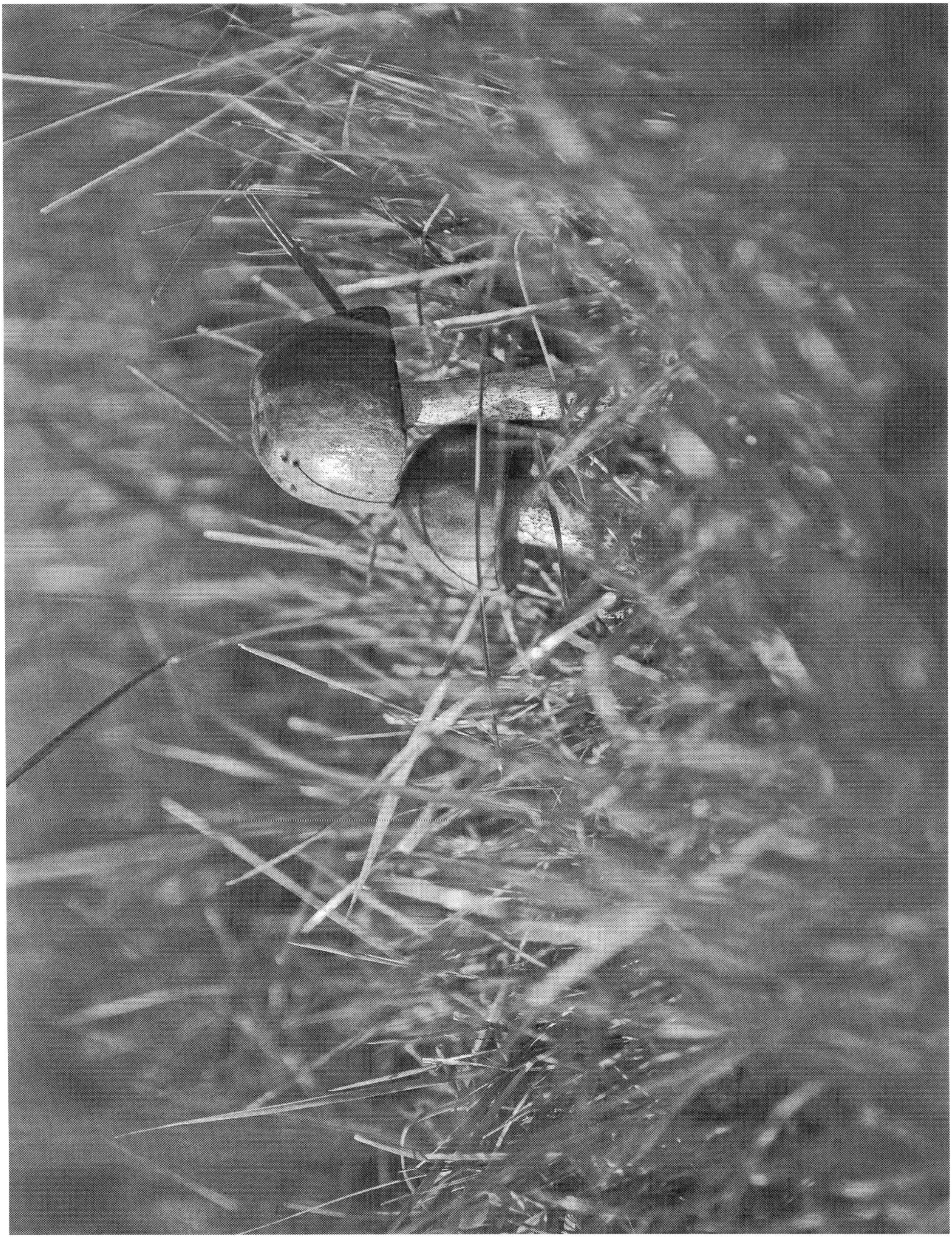

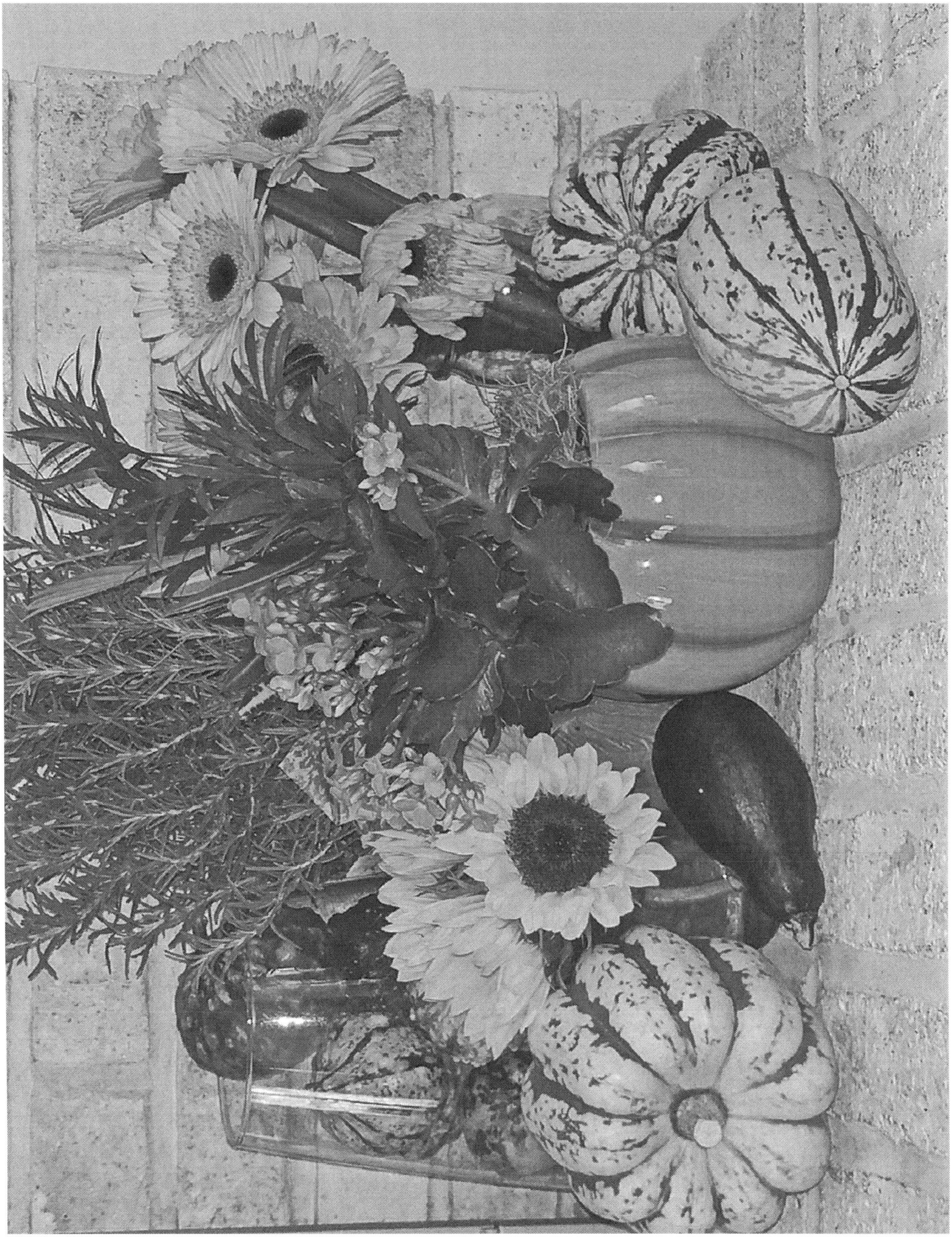

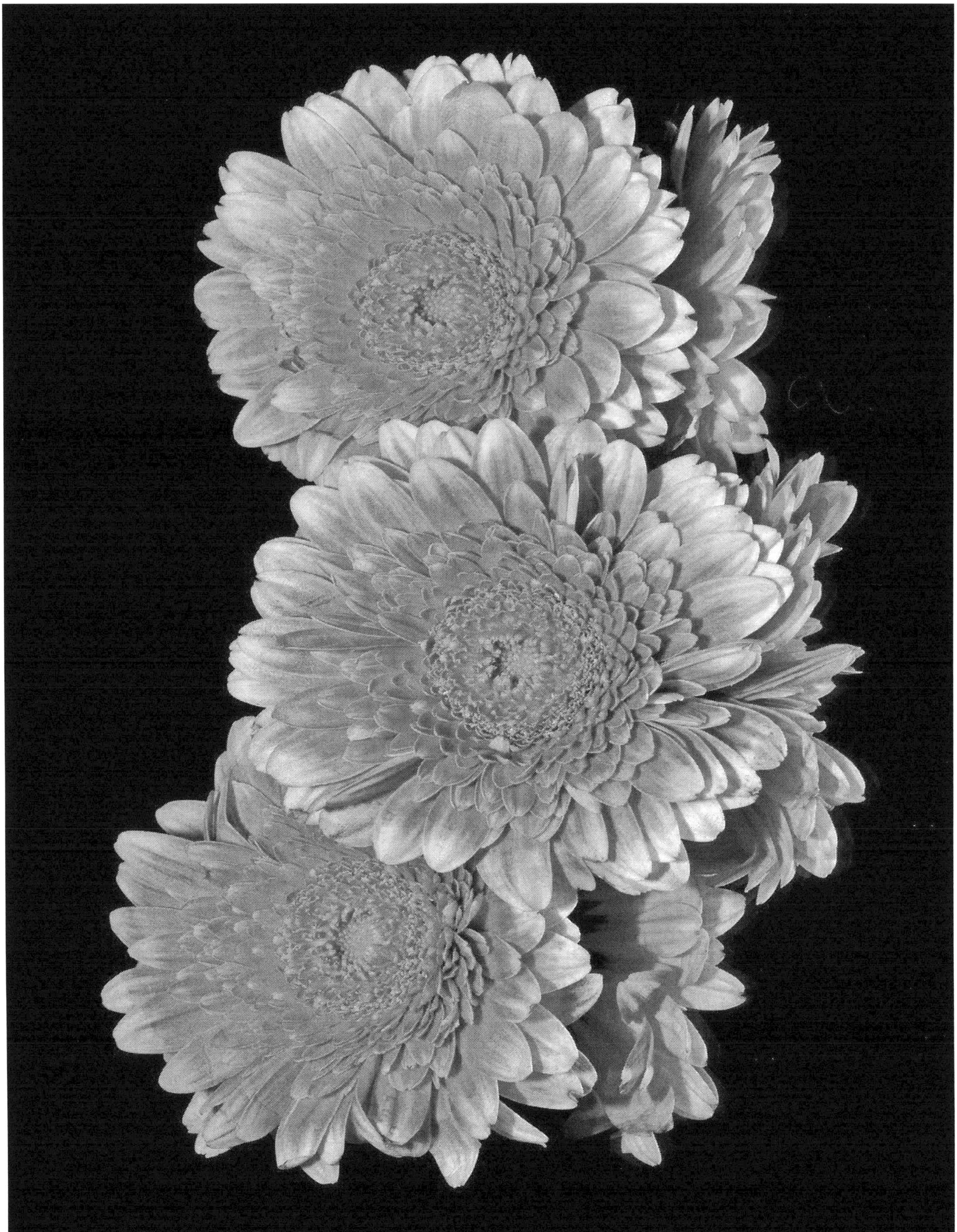

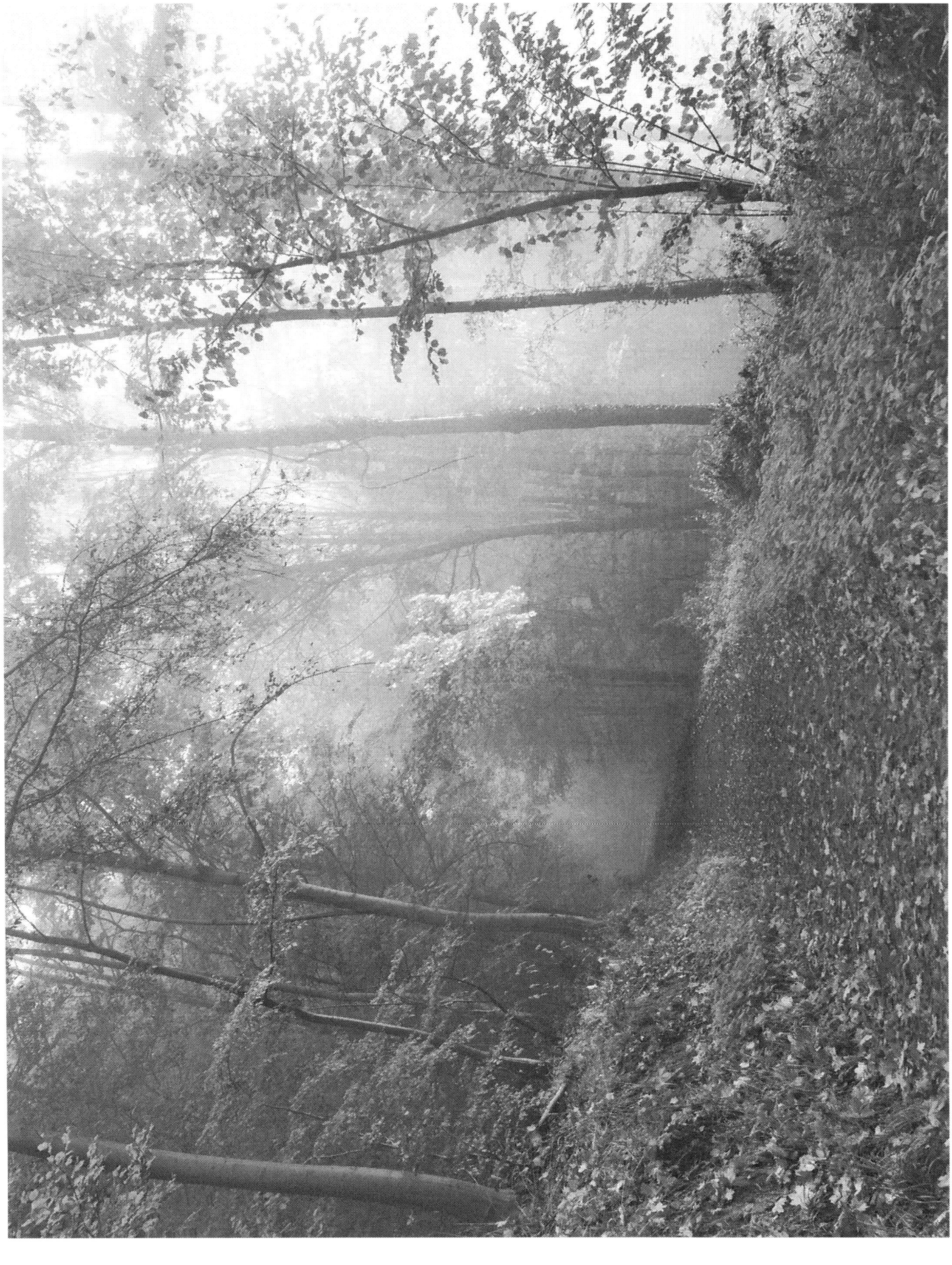

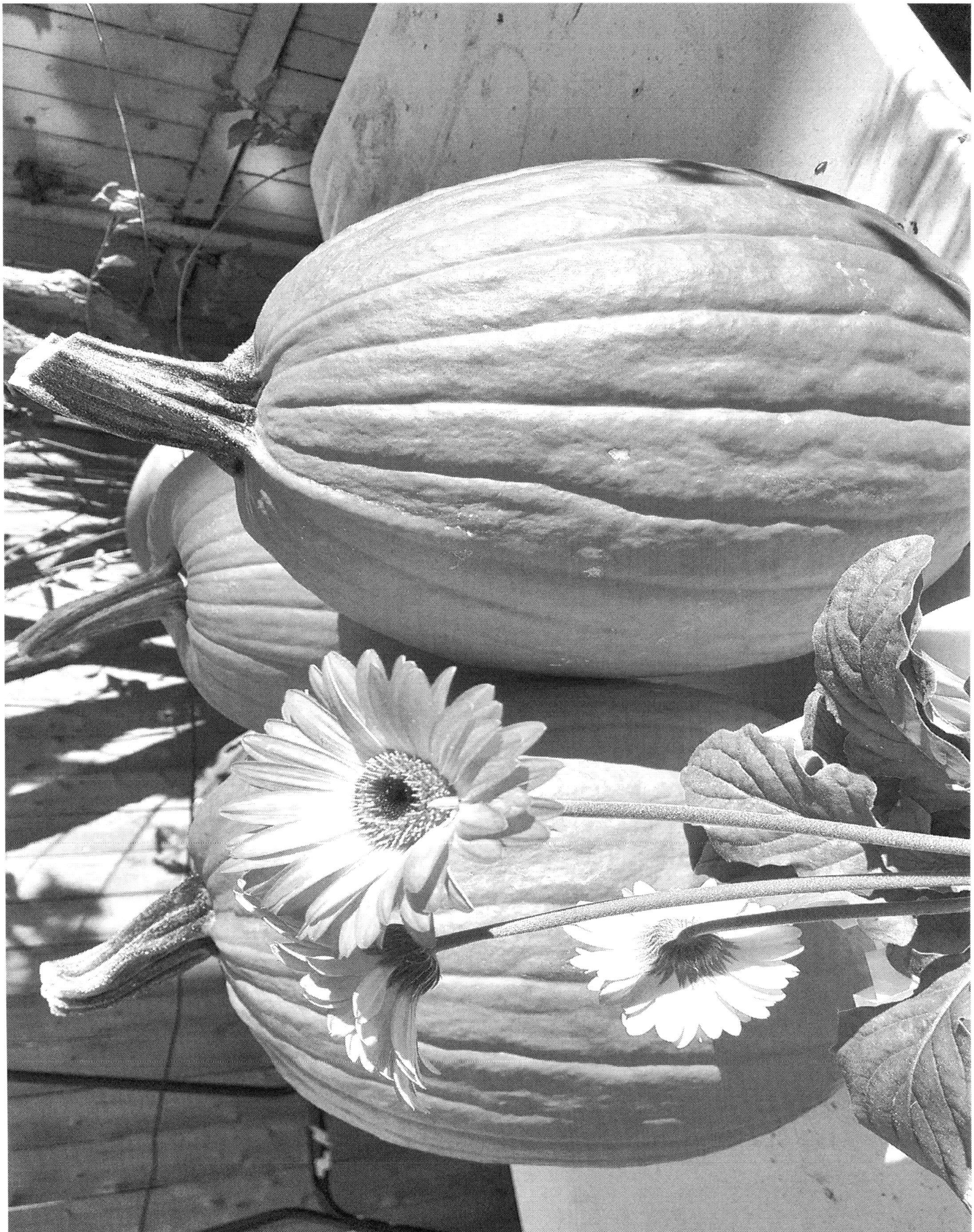

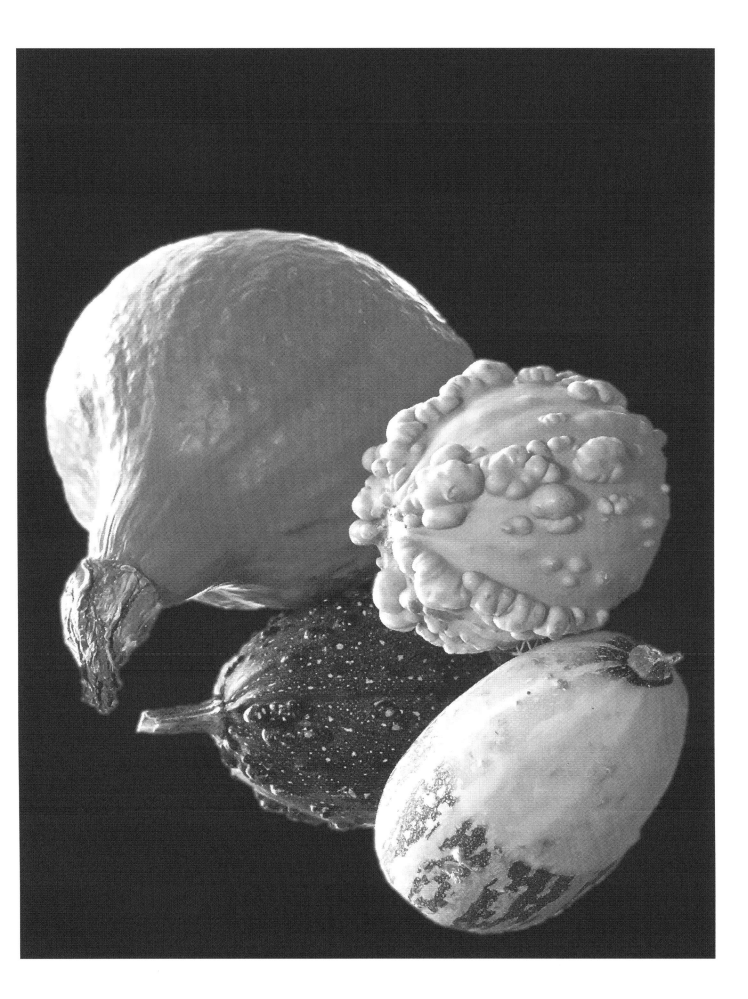

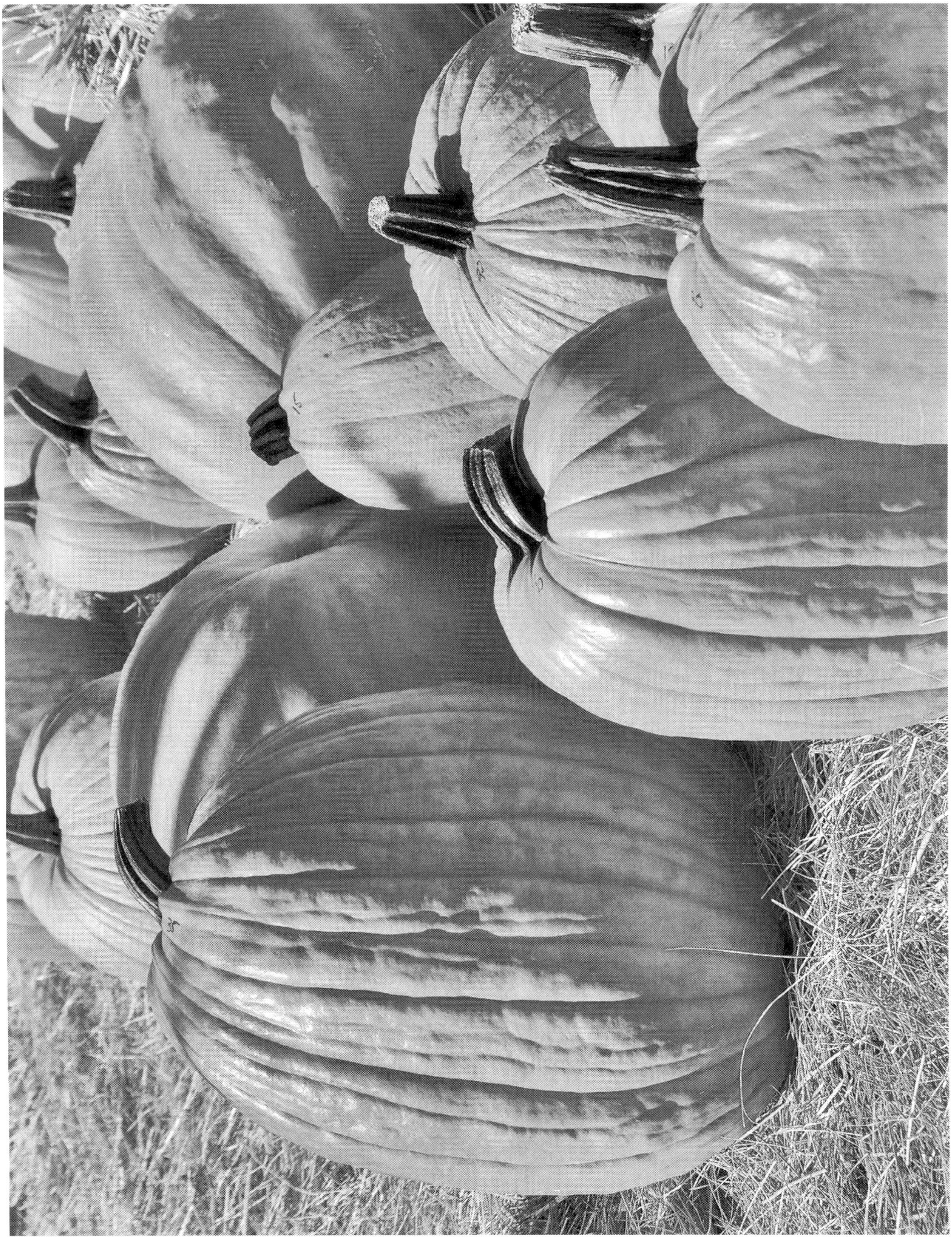

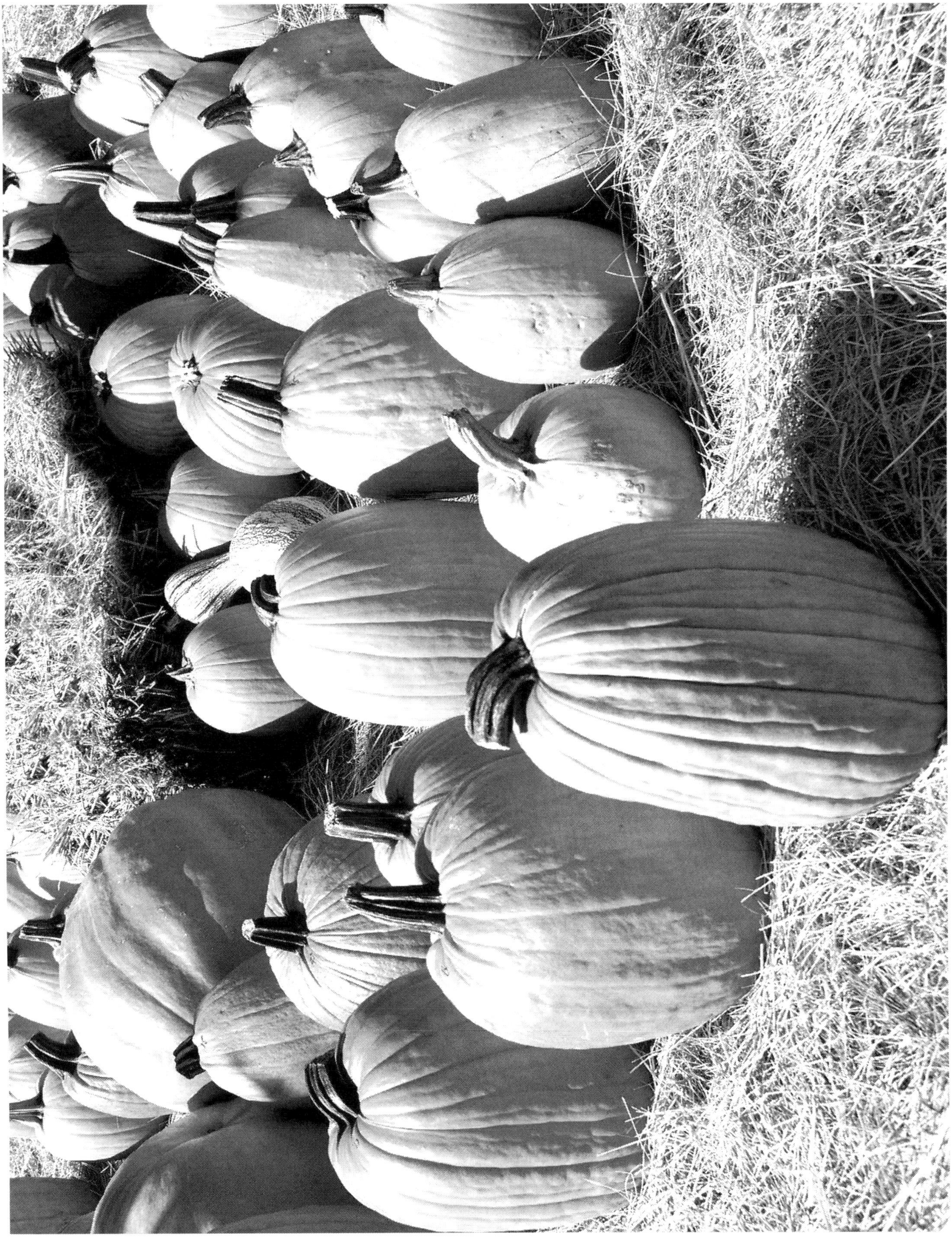

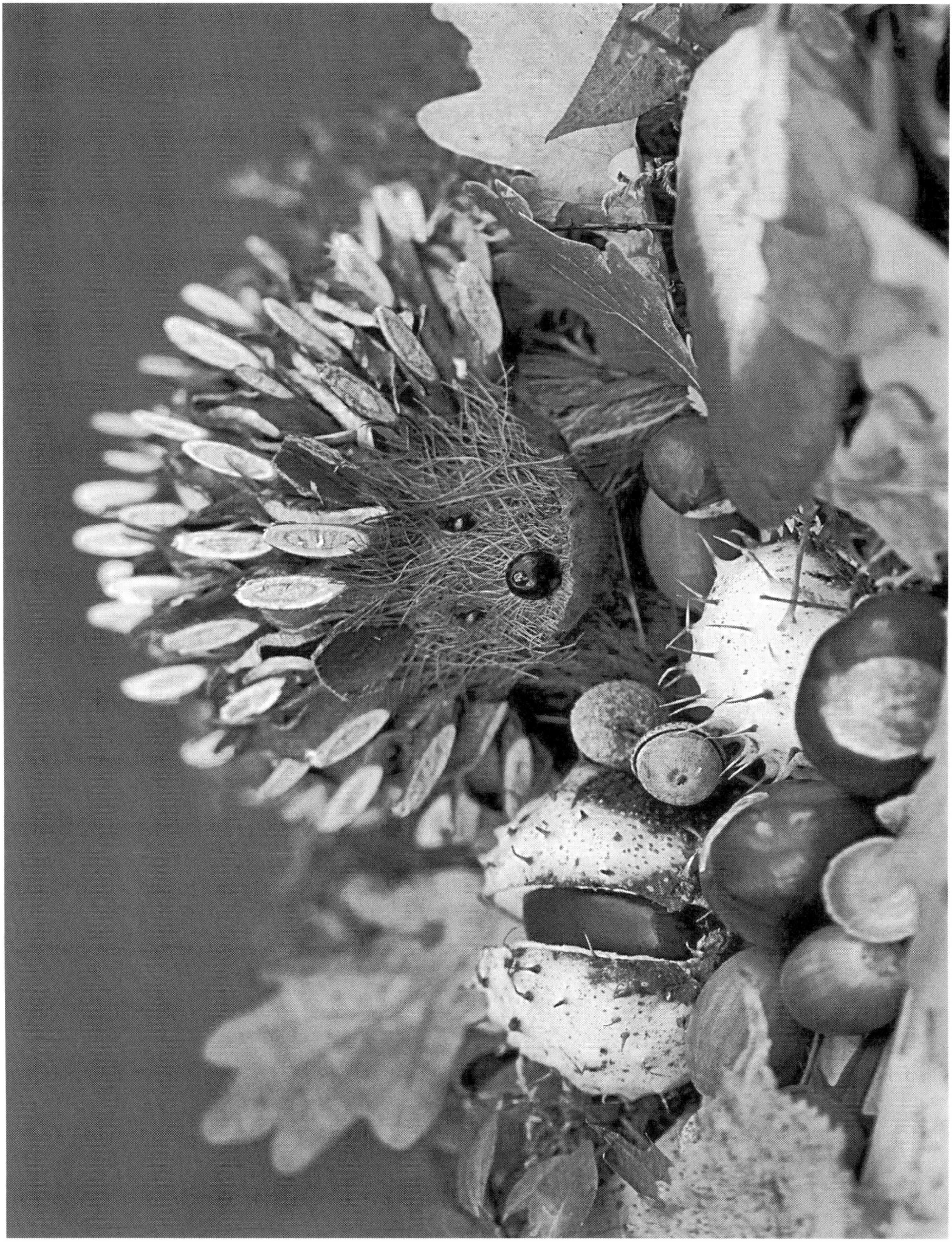

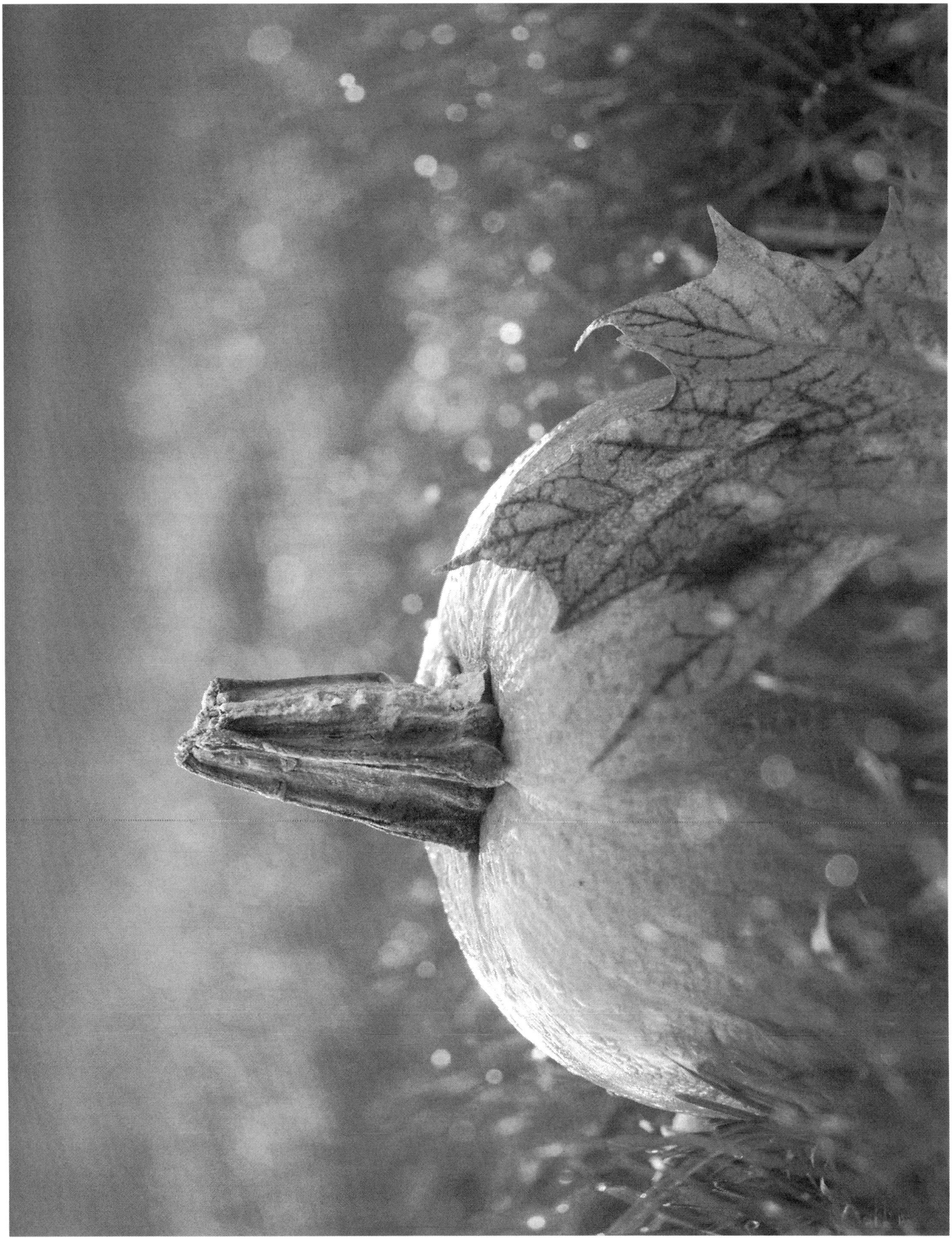

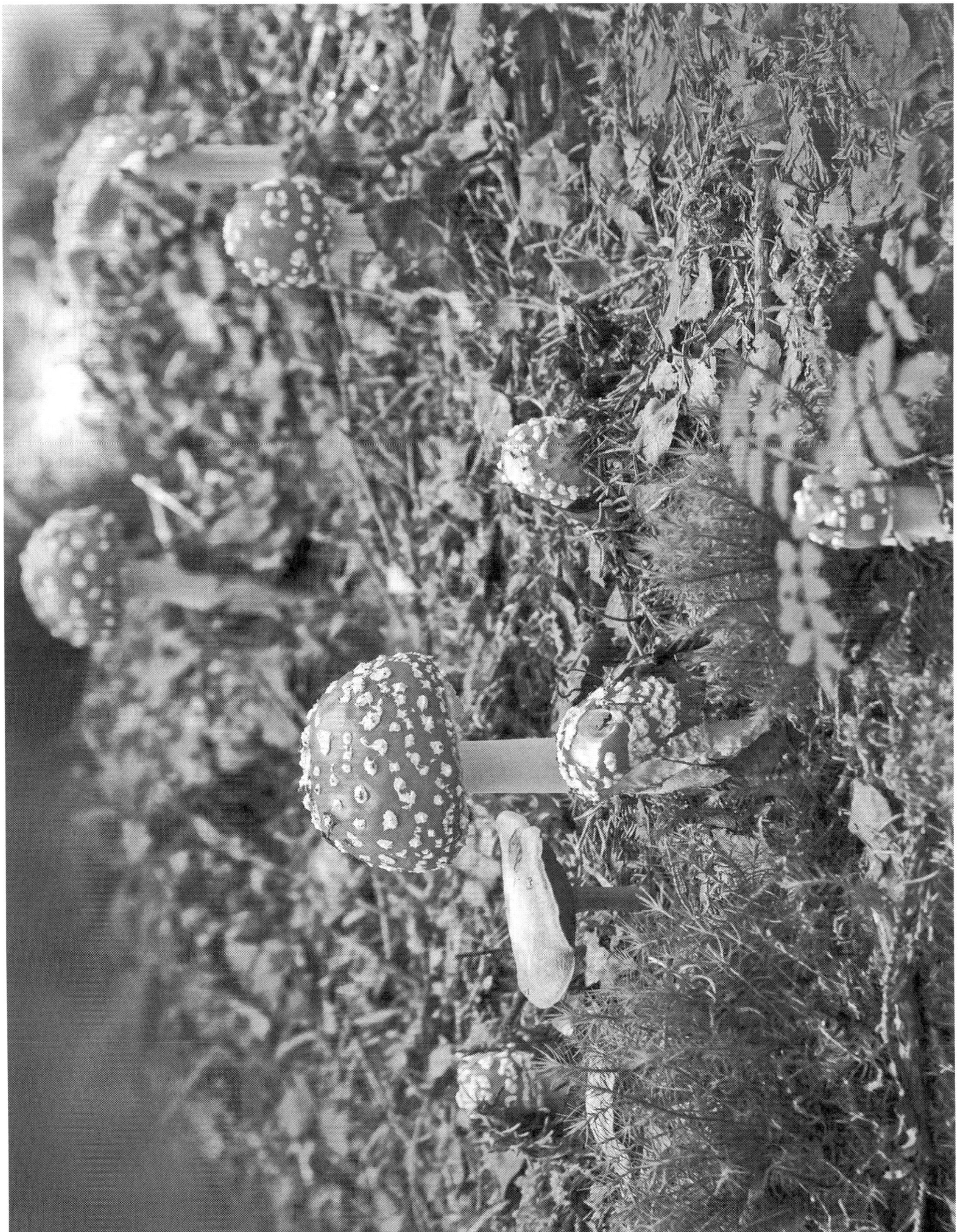